ABOUT THE AUTHOR

Patrick Chabal is Professor at King's College London. He trained in political science at Harvard, Columbia and Cambridge universities and has taught and researched in Africa, the USA and Europe. He writes broadly on the history, politics and culture of African countries and more generally on political theory. His publications include *Culture Troubles: Politics and the Interpretation of Meaning* (2006) with J.-P. Daloz; *Africa Works: Disorder as a Political Instrument* (1999) with J.-P. Daloz; *Power in Africa* (1992 and 1994); and *Amílcar Cabral: Revolutionary Leadership and People's War* (1982 and 2003).

WORLD POLITICAL THEORIES

World Political Theories will change the way we think about non-Western political ideas. Each book in the series looks at a particular political region, and how thinking about politics has developed there. In doing so, the books will ask how universal political theory actually is, and to what extent place makes a difference. Through looking at the historical development of political thinking, and at the ways in which it is being used and changing today, the books provide important context for understanding contemporary politics in Africa, the Middle East, East Asia and Latin America and introduce new ideas and challenges to conventional political theory.

AFRICA

The politics of suffering and smiling

PATRICK CHABAL

Zed Books
LONDON & NEW YORK

University of KwaZulu–Natal Press
PIETERMARITZBURG, SOUTH AFRICA

'Shuffering and Shmiling' is the actual title of
Fela Ransom Kuti's famous song of 1978

Africa: The Politics of Suffering and Smiling was first published in 2009 by:

in southern Africa, University of KwaZulu–Natal Press,
Private Bag XO1, Scottsville 3209, South Africa
www.ukznpress.co.za

in the rest of the world, Zed Books Ltd, 7 Cynthia Street, London N1 9JF, UK
and Room 400, 175 Fifth Avenue, New York, NY 10010, USA
www.zedbooks.co.uk

Designed and typeset in Monotype Joanna by illuminati, Grosmont,
www.illuminatibooks.co.uk
Cover designed by Lucy Morton @ illuminati
Printed and bound in the EU by Gutenberg Press Ltd

Distributed in the USA exclusively by Palgrave Macmillan,
a division of St Martin's Press, LLC, 175 Fifth Avenue, New York, NY 10010

A catalogue record for this book is available from the British Library
Library of Congress Cataloging in Publication Data available

ISBN   978 1 84277 908 8 Hb (Zed Books)
ISBN   978 1 84277 909 5 Pb (Zed Books)

ISBN   978 1 86914 163 9 (University of KwaZulu–Natal Press)

For Farzana and Emile

Contents

Preface

This book is an attempt to tackle post-colonial politics in Africa from a different angle. Different in that it does not focus on the standard questions of comparative politics: state, civil society, elites, political economy, ethnicity, development, corruption, international relations, and so on. It tries instead to get at the stuff of politics from below, or rather from within. Of course, this is a tall order. These are not questions that can be answered 'objectively', once and for all. There is a very strong personal and subjective aspect to my enterprise, as there is for all those who study Africa. But there is also a very pragmatic side: put at its simplest, does my analysis of African post-colonial politics provide new insights?

The choice of topics discussed in the book's seven chapters draws on my reading of the situation on the ground today and my reading of the material offered to explain that situation. Under the guise of a survey of those aspects of life that affect most people most of the time, I offer a plan of work that captures some of the key aspects of contemporary African societies. I recognise that others might have made a different choice. This is merely my current ordering of what I think matters. But there is logic to the structure of the book.

The chapters are meant to capture the cycle of individual and communal lives, from birth to death, and to give importance to those areas I believe to be of greatest importance in today's Africa. This is not, therefore, a general blueprint for the study of politics in Africa. It is a contextually drawn framework for the study of some of the most relevant questions about power. Nor am I making any claim for its continued relevance over time. It may be that in a decade or two it will be necessary to ask different questions and to provide distinct conceptual orderings. This is very much how it should be.

For now, let me explain why I have organised the book in this way. My primary concern has been to devise a scheme that would not be driven, either theoretically or conceptually, by the standard methodologies applied to African politics. Not because they are without merit but simply because I think they have reached their limits – by which I mean that they are no longer telling us anything new. We need to try to think afresh. So the idea here is to get at politics indirectly, through an investigation of how it is played out in these key areas of human existence.

Stepping out of the field of comparative politics has forced me onto other terrains, other disciplines, most notably anthropology. I make no apology for this but I do recognise that it implies different agendas and brings with it other constraints. If I find the anthropological angle useful it is because it compels me to re-examine familiar issues through a different lens. But there is also much of interest in culture, literature and religious studies, which I have used extensively.

This does not mean I neglect other approaches in the social sciences. For example, I am not arguing that studying Africa's place in the current world economic system is superfluous. On the contrary. But there is today a vast literature on such questions as international political economy and globalisation – from which the student of Africa can choose the most plausible approach. Here, however, I link the analysis of the economy to outside factors only as they play themselves out in the everyday lives of African men and women. I leave the bigger picture to others.

My second objective has been to offer an interpretation of African politics that worked my 'subjective' readings into a coherent analytical whole – or, to put it another way, that made my standpoint readable. By choosing an unorthodox approach, I have made it easier both to assess and to contest it. I happen to believe my approach helps us to get closer to an understanding of politics in Africa but I want to invite discussion of its limitations. Since in the social sciences the advancement of knowledge is both incremental and disorderly, my method should facilitate constructive debate. My hope, therefore, is that this book will be measured by how insightful an account it provides of actual politics – not how it stands against pre-set theories.

Lastly, my intention has been to bring back people into politics. There is nothing wrong with big questions and the study of causalities, but we tend easily to forget human beings in our sociological enquiries and regression analyses. I want here to fix my camera at eye level and engage with politics as it is played out in everyday life. I have eschewed the macro for the micro, the high for the low, and the elite for the ordinary. Ideally, I would like to answer the question of what politics means for people who are not political actors. This is probably beyond the competence of any one individual, especially an outsider. But I hope the attempt to address that question can make a difference to our understanding of contemporary African societies.

Let me make two final remarks. First, I shall refer in the following chapters to the current literature on African politics only as required. Thus, the book does not attempt to present a representative summary of existing Africanist political science, which is extensive. It will instead engage critically with the present *corpus*, as appropriate.[1] In my view, there is little to be gained by making claims of superiority in this respect. What matters is to explain why certain arguments are more plausible than others and why. Second, throughout the

---

1. I have deliberately omitted footnotes, except where indispensable. Instead, the bibliography provides reference to some of the literature I have found useful. However, this bibliography is neither exhaustive nor intended to be representative of any particular Africanist discipline.

book I shall refer to Africanists, by which I mean both African and non-African students of Africa. If I speak more systematically of Western Africanists it is merely because I am one. But the book is intended as a dialogue with our African colleagues, whether they agree with my approach or not. The point is not artificially to agree or disagree but to engage in meaningful and critical discussion, which I wholeheartedly invite.

I want to thank Ellen Hallsworth, who encouraged me to write this book. I should like to acknowledge the Institute for Advanced Study, Princeton, which offered me membership during the academic year 2006–07 and provided the most extraordinarily agreeable setting for the reading and thinking that went into the book. Here, I would like especially to record my debt of gratitude to Clifford Geertz, who sadly died whilst I was in residence, and to Joan Scott, who responded generously to my somewhat unreasonable requests for feedback. I am also particularly grateful to David Scott for coruscating intellectual debate; although we may not always have found agreement, he forced me to think harder and pushed me to be sharper. I should like to give warm thanks to John Lonsdale, for continued critical support, and to Miguel Cabrera for a most productive academic dialogue. I thank Steven Feierman and Sandra Barnes for friendship, support and wisdom. I also learnt a great deal during my conversations with Herman Bennett, Karen Blu, Kristen Ghodsee, Rosalind Morris, Jennifer Pitts, Benjamin Schmidt and Lisa Wedeen. As ever, I am grateful to my departmental colleagues for providing a congenial atmosphere particularly conducive to research. Finally, I should like to thank the London School of Economics for asking me to give the Obi Igwara Memorial Lecture, in which I presented a book chapter that was followed by a fruitful discussion. But I owe most to Farzana and Emile, to whom this book is dedicated, since they brought meaning, humanity and insight to what I was doing.

Introduction

The attempt to write a political theory of Africa immediately faces two intractable issues. The first has to do with the question of what a political theory of any particular region of the world might mean. The second is linked to the fact that this region of the world happens to be Africa. I will address these two questions systematically throughout the book but I begin with a short general discussion.

Pleasant as it would be to believe that these issues could be tackled in a broadly consensual way, the fact is that the study of African politics is deeply contentious. This is not just because there is no agreement on what might constitute the key questions that need answering but also, and perhaps primarily, because the political analysis of the continent arouses strong emotions, which often have little to do with the matter at hand. In some strange ways the study of Africa often appears *sui generis* or uniquely different, an issue it is useful to confront squarely from the outset.

Here I want merely to stress the fact that it is well nigh impossible to discuss African politics without venturing onto the difficult terrain of normative and personal considerations. Africans and Africanists are often locked into a world of shadow boxing, where issues of substance are linked to arguments about standpoint, origin, authority and subjectivities. The result is that debates about analysis, theory and interpretation are also debates about the validity, and even legitimacy, of the utterances pronounced by those who study the continent. Of course, this is inherent in the study of the 'other' – as all anthropologists know. Yet, it would be disingenuous to ignore the fact that it is a more particularly persistent issue when it comes to Africa. I now turn to the two issues I raised above: (i) what does it mean to offer a political theory of a particular region of the world? (ii) what are the specific problems attached to the study of Africa as a region?

THE USES OF POLITICAL THEORY

Tackling this question in a constructive way demands that we address two separate problems. One is whether an agenda in terms of political theory is best suited to accounting for politics in Africa. The other has to do with whether it is possible to think in terms of the political theory of a region and, if it is, whether it is desirable. These are both complicated questions and I limit my discussion only to what is relevant to this book. Indeed, my standpoint throughout is resolutely 'pragmatic': I favour what serves to provide insight over theoretical ambition. Or, to put it another way, theory is only deployed where it clearly serves the purpose of offering an account of African politics that is enlightening. Therefore, my aim is not to construct a political theory of Africa but only to try to theorise politics in Africa – that is, to engage in the theoretical discussions that can provide added value to our understanding of how power is exercised on the continent. Of particular acuity here are the questions of whether prevailing notions of theory are ethnocentric and whether existing theories of comparative politics are suited to the study of Africa.

There is no reason in principle to argue that 'theory' is ethnocentric if the definition of theory is a general one, such as the systematic organisation of knowledge. However, that is too simple an approach. Theory does not stand in a vacuum; it is constructed within historically bounded contexts and it is applied in specific ways. Furthermore, the very meaning of theory is problematic since it implies a particular way of 'explaining' that derives from a Western tradition of rationality and scientific endeavour, which originates in the Enlightenment. In the longer term it may well be necessary to recast our approach to what theory is supposed to imply in such a radical fashion as to invalidate much of our current scholarly work.[1]

For now I want to stress that present-day social science assumes that the concept of theory is generally intended to connote a particular set of articulated causalities, especially related to issues of development or progress. Therefore, to engage in a discussion of a 'political theory of Africa' is necessarily to take up the issue of comparative politics – and this for two reasons. One is that modern political theory as it is practised in Western academic departments is usually understood either as an attempt to conceptualise the evolution of politics in Western societies or as a study of Western political thought. The other is that any attempt to develop a political theory to make sense of other societies is necessarily an attempt to compare the West and the non-West.

The political theories that are relevant to the study of post-colonial Africa fall into distinct, largely chronological, categories: development, Marxist, dependency, socialist, indigenous, neo-patrimonial and democratic. Although such classification is somewhat simplistic, and these categories are not neatly delineated with absolute precision, and in some cases overlap, they do represent the main frameworks of analysis and debate since Africa became independent. I've discussed these theories in detail elsewhere,[2] so I focus here on what they entail as political theories of Africa. I want especially to highlight the interpretative and causal differences between these approaches as well as the assumptions they share.

---

1. As I will do in my next book, *Western Rationality after Post-Colonialism*.
2. Chabal, 1994, Part I.

Theories of development, whatever their guise, made two clear assumptions: the first was that there is a path to (economic and political) development, which all countries follow, if in different ways; the second was that Africa is merely behind on that path but that it will eventually catch up. Therefore, the role of theory was to identify those factors that hindered or facilitated the onward march of progress, which independence was supposed to have made possible. The questions asked were intended to assess the extent to which political processes and economic policies favoured the 'natural' development of the continent that would follow its freeing from the colonial yoke. Such theories, which must be set within their Cold War context, were thus teleological and rested on well-understood causalities: economic growth would facilitate a type of socio-political change, which in turn would enable the gradual emergence of more democratic polities.

Marxist (or neo-Marxist) and dependency theories can be seen as mirror images of development theories in that they were also teleological and also offered clear causal links. Whereas the former saw in the spread of capitalism and the workings of competitive politics the template for 'development', the latter considered that socialism and the vanguard party-state would drive 'progress' forward. However, this broad church was divided between those who believed that socialist solidarity was necessary and those who argued that socialist autarchy was the solution. Hence, some advanced the need for more capitalist penetration of African economies while others advocated instead a national economic development plan that would cut off dependence on the world market and thus break the vicious circle of underdevelopment capitalism brought about.

What I call 'indigenous' theories refer to the diverse, and not always compatible, approaches that stemmed from a local rather than universal conceptualisation of African politics. These range from the once influential debate about African socialism to the call for an 'authentic' African development, by way of an argument that one-party or no-party politics are the most appropriate for Africa.

These theories derive in part from a vast intellectual and historical scholarship, which sought to refocus history and social sciences within a more genuinely African perspective. They relate in part to claims that Africa had a much more central place in the development of the modern world than Western theories allow. These theories also question the universal validity of the equation often made between modernisation and Westernisation.

Briefly, I would like to bring out both the origins and the relevance of those 'indigenous' theories. Going as far back as pan-Africanism and Négritude, there has always been in Africa a strong vision of what made the continent different. Much as he was later lambasted for his essentialist views of Africans, Senghor certainly made manifest in his writings aspects of African culture and art that resonate to this day. Although in his political practice Senghor was a very conventional politician, it cannot be denied that he was able effectively to combine a commitment to a modern notion of economic development and an astute understanding of the local factors that were relevant to political success in Senegal. His argument is interesting in part because it was articulated with such brio, even if Négritude failed to spawn a theoretical progeny.

However, there are current echoes of the argument about African specificities. Museveni's view that the continent must avoid party politics is not a mere quirk. It rests on a well thought-out argument that, in present circumstances, multiparty politics will inevitably be channelled through and exacerbate ethnic conflict. This political theory of Africa thus rejects the assumption that political development must necessarily follow the contemporary Western model. Equally, the current Ethiopian regime's insistence on organising political representation on an ethnic basis derives from a notion of the 'natural' organisation of African peoples in today's Africa – even if, like Museveni's template, it can also be seen as self-serving. More broadly, there is a school of thought arguing that ethnicity in Africa is more than mere relic from the past. It is at the heart of the everyday realities of morality, accountability and representation and as such needs to form the bedrock of any realistic political theory of the continent.[3]

What I group under neo-patrimonial theories includes a fairly wide range of distinct approaches, which all share the view that a conceptualisation of local factors is critical to the understanding of African politics. Here there are two contrasting starting points. One is that what matters most is the historical working out of patterns of universal development as applied to Africa. The other is that indigenous socio-economic and cultural features have determining influence over the exercise of power in Africa. Of course, these are fundamental differences that ought not to be brushed aside but I am concerned here to stress why both converge in their analysis of contemporary African politics, as can be seen in their discussion of the state. The former argues that the transplantation of the Western state has failed to take root, implying thereby that it was the wrong model. The latter adduces that the African state necessarily reflects the patrimonial nature of local politics. The upshot is not dissimilar: the state is not institutionally functional.

Democratic theory, which is virtually hegemonic today, harks back to a straightforward developmental approach that is reminiscent of earlier modernisation models. Sustained by a vision of liberal democracy as the only viable model of modern politics, this theory interprets the present blossoming of multiparty elections in Africa as the early phase of an ineluctable move towards democratisation. Rooted in institutionalist notions of political change, it rests on the supposition that the practices of democratic elections will eventually result in the emergence of a democratic political 'culture'. Like earlier democratic theories, it is universalist, teleological and steeped in a notion of modernisation as a variant of Westernisation.

I will not here assess the extent to which these various theories are ethnocentric since the book itself provides the elements needed for an appreciation of how justified or relevant this concern is.

---

3. Lonsdale, 1995, 2003.

Instead, I want to look more closely at the notion of agency, which has become today one of the most influential approaches in the political analysis of Africa.

THE QUESTION OF AGENCY

This first question is, why has the notion of agency acquired such a prominent place in the current social science discourse on Africa? What, in any event, does agency mean or, perhaps more concretely, how does the concept help us better understand African realities at the beginning of the twenty-first century? What, if any, are the connections between the focus on agency and the current international order, which is commonly thought to be detrimental to Africa?

Agency is usually understood as directed, meaningful, intentional and self-reflective social action. It comes out of a long-standing debate about the respective importance of structure and individual action in social change. That debate has its roots in two distinct genealogies. The first has to do with a number of shifts in the social sciences since the 1960s. The second is linked to the evolving situation in Africa, which most analysts frame today in terms of the impact of globalisation on the continent. The dominance after the Second World War of Marxist, neo-Marxist, teleological or structuralist approaches to the study of society began to be questioned in the 1960s. However, it was not until the 1970s that its supremacy was challenged. Foucault and Habermas, each in his very different epistemological manner, initiated a number of critiques, which were eventually to change the face of the social sciences. These changes began to influence the way Africanists went about their business.

There were at least two important shifts in history and the social sciences, which had a deep impact on the question of agency. On the one hand, the rise of cultural history and the linguistic turn have led to a reassessment of historiography. This has opened up a vast transformation in the 'theory' of history, particularly in areas such as feminism and post-colonial studies. On the other hand, the social sciences themselves have undergone a double shift: the historical and linguistic turns. These have brought about a focus on subjectivity, discourse and deconstruction. That challenge to structuralism and teleology, in history and the social sciences, recast the question of agency as well as the matter of causality.

The move away from the structural determinant of social action took a long time and proceeded unevenly. Where African Studies are concerned, the 1960s and 1970s were a period during which theories of (economic and political) development combined to suggest that the putting in place of the right structures and the execution of the right policies would result in progress. The disagreements concerned the question of whether capitalist or socialist frameworks were the most powerful engines of modernisation. Whether capitalist or socialist, the theories deployed all took it for granted that agency was directly conditioned by the economic, political and social constraints extant in each particular society and within the global economic order. The question was not, therefore, whether different agency might result in different outcomes but how agency could best be applied to purposeful social action within the structural framework that determined the range of possible options. Agency, then, was subordinated to structure within the context of an understanding of historical causality that suffered little dissent.

Although the move away from such a conceptual framework began to gather momentum in the 1960s, the particular situation of Africa prevented this shift from having decisive analytical purchase until the 1980s. If the gradual emergence of a discourse of agency masks any clear epistemological break, it is important to set the debate in some historical context. It is in fact the fall of the Berlin Wall, along with the collapse of Communism in the Soviet Union and Eastern Europe, which helped to bring back subjectivity and agency in the analysis of social and political action. For example, the modern resurgence of civil society as a social entity with decisive influence on the political transformation of modern polities derives from an analysis of the East European transitions to democracy that gives pride of place to agency.

The post-Communist context encouraged the flowering of theories of modernisation, which placed the strong individualism of liberal democracy and the decisive role of the market at the heart of political and economic change – in Africa as in the rest of the world. It is within this setting that democratisation washed over Africa and began to redefine the terms of the discussion on development. Agency is in this way the link between democracy and the market, both of which privilege an analysis of society in terms of the empowered individual endowed with social, political and economic rights.

The situation in Africa at the time when the entwined discourses on democracy and market gained ascendancy was that of extreme economic and political crisis. At the same time, the end of the Cold War and the concern in the West for the evolution of the former Communist states made it much more difficult for African countries to get the aid on which their very survival depended. So it was that a fundamental rethinking of the African predicament began to take shape. So it was too that the discourse about Africa began to change.

The recognition of the limited success (or outright failure) of the benign 'paternalism' that had presided over the imposition of structural adjustment programmes – the thinking being that African governments had to be taught how to manage their economy for the purpose of development – was linked to a new vision of African agency. This vision had its origins in two separate though clearly interrelated processes. One was the extent of social mobilisation that had led to the revolt against the one-party state and ushered in competitive politics in most African countries. This hinted both at the powerful effects of 'civil society' as a key driver of change and at the potential for positive transition inherent in democracy. The other was the realisation that there were myriad informal social, economic and political activities that demonstrated the ability of Africans to survive the catastrophic conditions under which they were compelled to live. This extraordinary dynamism and ingenuity suggested that once the heavy hand of the state had been removed there would be scope for genuine developmental progress.

Since the early 1990s, therefore, there has emerged a two-strand discourse on agency. One has tapped into the new aid ideology of providing support to civil society at the local level – a role devolved to (foreign and domestic) NGOs or civil society organisations (CSOs). The other has linked with the idea that development would require the combined efforts of individuals: informal ingenuity would have to be channelled into formal productive activities that would sustain economic growth. This largely foreign vision of the new Africa was reinforced by the discourse of African politicians who now berated the failures of the one-party state model of development and promised to facilitate both political reform and market-friendly policies.

The new discourse on Africa was sealed in the two key documents of the turn of the century: NEPAD and the Millennium Development Goals (MDG) – one the mirror image of the other. The subtext was clear: help yourself and the world will help you. The new dispensation was predicated on the force of agency: directed African action would, with the help of the outside world, bring forth greater political accountability, more development and a reduction in poverty. The G8 summit in 2005 finalised this compact with Africa.

Yet another powerful strand in the genealogy of the discourse on agency has been the need, among Africans and Africanists alike, to counter the mood of Afro-pessimism, which descended over the continent in the 1980s and has hardly lifted since. Many hoped to move away from the perspective of Africa as victim and give pride of place to African initiative. This was a deliberate attempt to counter those approaches that stressed the structural features of African societies, most particularly neo-patrimonialism, as being the main factors in the present crisis. The claim made by those who favoured agency was that a focus on what was being achieved, instead of what had failed, would highlight the local ways in which African actors had managed to cope with the burden of weak/failed states and the pressures of globalisation. Centring attention on agency would change the questions we asked about African societies.

This approach to the notion of agency points to the limits of much Africanist social science. It argues that existing paradigms have failed to explain contemporary Africa, casting it into an everlasting vicious circle of impotence. Therefore, there is a need to provide an analytical framework that does justice to the processes of social change *actually* taking place in Africa today. Agency has now become a powerful concept, which informs not just scholarship but also policymaking. It contributes to new approaches in development aid that have immediate consequences for Africa. Perhaps it is in the process of becoming the new orthodoxy.

However, a closer look at the concept of agency in Africa reveals an ambiguity at its very core. On the one hand, the notion has arisen from epistemological changes in the social sciences, reflecting primarily Western, non-African, societies. On the other hand, it has emerged from the ground up as a category of analysis for the local African context. Although the word used is the same, it carries vastly different implications. The former centres on the recognition that in 'modern' societies the individual is deemed to be more of a free agent than in so-called 'traditional' societies. The very condition of 'modernity' is taken to be the vastness of the possibilities for individual social and political action – even if such freedom carries the danger of alienation. The latter suggests the ability of Africans to adapt to, and to process, modernity for their own purposes and in their own ways. It derives, therefore, from what is often dismissed as 'tradition'.

Of course, it is recognised that the absence of resources and opportunities influences the extent to which African men and women are able to act upon the environment in which they live. It is also admitted that African societies are not primarily atomistic in ways that would put a premium on the individual's intentional, purposeful and autonomous social action. For all these reservations, however, the notion of agency has taken a firm hold on Africanist social and political analysis. It is almost as if the incantation of agency ought eventually to create a firmer sense of individual potentialities in Africa today. So, how useful is the concept in the African context? I tackle this issue from two different angles. The first is to tease out the ways in which it forces us to ask different questions about what is happening on the continent. The second is to discuss the extent to which, as a mirror image of the notion of Afro-pessimism, it might not be inextricably bound with the causalities it seeks to undermine.

There is little doubt that concentrating on agency forces us to (re)consider the main questions we've been asking since independence. Instead of raising the issue of why Africa has not developed, we are directed to consider the extraordinary ways in which Africans have adapted to rapidly changing international circumstances. From a context in the 1960s when the Cold War was at its height and the formal colonial powers still had strong influence in their former territories to the present globalised world in which financial, communication and trade flows have accelerated, Africa's situation has evolved massively. A focus on the adjustments Africans have had to make to adapt to these global influences brings out the ability of both rulers and peoples to grasp the opportunities available to them and deploy them to purposeful effect. A few examples will make the point.

The agility demonstrated by African governments in maximising resource transfers within the radically different environments of the Cold War, structural adjustment and, today, rapid globalisation is truly impressive. Equally, the speed with which Africans have deployed the discourse and instruments of democracy to force greater accountability on their governors is remarkable. In another register, the ease with which Africans have adapted to the spread of the mobile phone and the Internet to facilitate commerce and migration is nothing short of astonishing. By the same token, the so-called informal economies have thrived in and beyond Africa. Finally, the rapid development of local NGOs as well as the increasingly organised and vocal intervention of CSOs demonstrate the potential for 'grassroots' movements to influence politics.

Concentrating attention on what has contributed to major political, social and economic changes in the last decade forces analysts to think again about the instruments they use to explain these events and processes. It compels us to revise any overall notion of causality we may have taken for granted by dint of the previous theoretical or conceptual frameworks. However, there is also another side to the issue of agency, which I want to examine now. The question here is how analytically relevant is the fact that the stress on agency is often an argument designed to rebut Afro-pessimism. From this angle, it seems to me that the stress on agency arises from two separate, though complementary, aspects of a particular approach to Africa. One is a deep and real concern that, contrary to the expectations of the early post-independence period, the continent has failed to develop. However this is to be explained, the situation demands an explanation. The other is the worry that globalisation, widely believed to have become the overriding factor in present world relations, is seriously detrimental to Africa – making it even less likely that the continent will be able finally to develop. I discuss how these two issues interact in the construction of current discourses on agency.

Explanations of the present situation in Africa fall into two, very unequal, categories. The first lays the blame on historical, environmental or structural factors, which range from neocolonialism to the nature of exports from the continent. Today, the main area of concern is the effect of globalisation on world trade. What these explanations all share is an emphasis on those conditions that affect Africa, which are outside local control. Africa is where it is because it suffers an unusually cruel combination of constraints. My point is not to assess the relative merit of these factors, all of which are relevant, but to highlight the way in which they emphasise causes that lie beyond agency: Africa is the victim of circumstances. Thus, such discourses point to the helplessness of those who are fated to live in that part of the world.

The other explanation, which stresses political factors, evokes instead processes and events that are largely rooted internally. Without neglecting any of the issues linked to the continent's fundamental 'extraversion', those who advocate a focus on the politics of Africa as the main cause of its crisis ask questions about the nature of accountability. Whether they speak of neo-patrimonialism or emphasise other political practices, they point to the fact that African political systems have failed to provide an environment within which it is possible for productive economic activities to flourish. This second line of attack, emphasising as it does the responsibility of African elites, can result in two diverging interpretations of politics in Africa.

One is to argue that the present condition of African states is the result of the working out of general historical processes in a local context – what is sometimes called the historicising of the state. The argument is that the transplantation of the colonial state into an environment that was not propitious *and* the historical development of that state in the post-colonial context have resulted in a political system that merely serves the interests of the elites. The other is that the present dereliction of the state in Africa is the result of the 'traditional' politics of Africa in the modern context of a continent that is sustained by outside aid. It is foreign assistance that makes it possible for the political elites to use the state in such a patrimonial fashion so as to stay in power.

Whilst the standard account of the deleterious effects of elite behaviour in Africa highlights their greed and dishonesty, these two interpretations point to the problem inherent in a political system that is blatantly averse to development. Both agree that the problem lies in a lack of real accountability but their diagnosis differs when it comes to agency. The first implies that the nature of politics in Africa is the result of the importation of a foreign state that is not suited to local conditions and that its adaptation has made possible the abuse of power. In this account, Africa is still the victim of a foreign intrusion. The second suggests that it is instead the transformation of political 'traditions' within the post-colonial context that is the heart of the problem. Here, the responsibility lies more squarely with elites that have fashioned a political system enabling them to abuse patrimonial forms of accountability.

And it is this second interpretation that is most often linked with Afro-pessimism *because* it implies that the problem lies with the singular adaptation of 'traditional' African forms of social and political relations to the modern world. Inevitably, the claim that it is the very socio-political and cultural foundations of African societies that may have the greater impact on the present crisis is taken to be an argument that the continent is *fated* never to manage to resolve its problems. This easily transmutes into the contention that the crisis is both inevitable and intractable, which implies that Africans lack agency – cursed as they are by their own institutions and traditions. Hence, the discourse of agency is in part an attempt to combat the ominous causalities of what is called Afro-pessimism.

Whilst it is reasonable that Africanists should seek to understand how Africans are adapting and succeeding in the modern world – how indeed they are domesticating modernity – it is important to bear in mind that such a normative approach is by no means devoid of analytical risks. My point is obviously not to decry the very useful, and insightful, emphasis given to the multiple ways in which Africans cope with the painful pangs of modernisation. It is instead to point to the fact that what lies behind the use of the notion of agency is rather more complicated than at first appears. Far from being an entirely novel conceptualisation, it is in fact merely a way of saying that Africans manage to cope in the adverse circumstances of a systemic condition in which development is not really on the agenda.

Yet, too relentless a focus on agency could also be seen as a way of avoiding telling the 'tragic' history of the continent, which the Nigerian songwriter Fela Kuti called *suffering and smiling*. It is a story that we outsiders find difficult to comprehend or with which we do not want to deal. But it is that story the present book seeks to address – not to rehearse yet again the fact that Africa is the 'victim' of history but to honour the day-to-day lives of those who strive to maintain human dignity in the face of overwhelming odds. The discussion of agency is thus a natural introduction to my own approach to the analysis of politics in contemporary Africa.

THE INTERPRETATION OF POST-COLONIAL POLITICS

The study of politics is concerned with power. It normally starts from things as they are supposed to be: individuals competing for resources within a given socio-economic framework. But perhaps this is the problem: what we set out to discover is what we know already because we have a sense of how the political system works. What we need to do is to come to the question of politics from a different angle – one that enables us to cast a different light on what is happening, for it is the light we cast, the questions we ask, which ultimately determines what we see.

It is in my view the enduring curse of the study of Africa that we, outsiders, have thought it necessary to seek in that continent confirmation of the theories we employ most readily in the analysis of our own societies. Of course, this has been done for good reasons. Given the history of the relationship between Africa and the West, it has become necessary to demonstrate that we apply to the continent the same norms, values and thus theories – lest we be seen to 'exoticise' the continent. However, the consequence of this state of affairs has been a tendency to be more concerned with approach than with content. *How* we do things matters more than *what* we do.

In this book I want to try to move away from this standpoint, useful as it has been in generating knowledge about Africa, and deploy a framework of analysis that may enlighten us in a different way. This is not to deny the validity of existing political theories, or to belittle their success in helping to explain politics in Africa. It is simply an attempt to think differently about old questions, to explore the possibility that there are other ways of understanding the logics and causalities with which we are confronted; other ways of making sense of what we see.

This is not entirely an arbitrary exercise since I believe that one of the chief impediments to our analysis of African politics is the filter that clouds our gaze – a filter that materialises from our assumptions about the workings of society, economy and polity. Mine is not an argument for an exclusivist and specialist Area Studies approach to Africa. Nor is it a plea for locally derived concepts and theories, based on the claim that reality on the continent defies classification. Even less should it be seen as an 'essentialised' figment of the Western imagination. I want to try to write about the Africa that stands before our eyes.[4]

Therefore this book will derive from an empirical study of realities that are all too often cast in the light of 'difference'. The issue is not whether Africa is 'different' (from which vantage point does one assess difference in any case?) but rather how the realities of the lives of those who live there affect the workings of politics. This is an approach that is as valid for Africa as it would be for any other part of the world and is as far removed from the particularistic slant as can reasonably be expected. And yet it will immediately raise three questions – questions that are more acute about Africa than about other areas, not because Africa is *effectively* more different but because *we* tend to approach it more differently.

The first has to do with the validity of the Western gaze on Africa. The second concerns the legacy of colonial scholarship on the continent. The last turns around the justification for generalising about such a huge geographical area with such diverse environment and populations. I take these in turn and explain why the answer to these questions has been deeply vitiated by the notion of 'difference'. This also leads me to make a few remarks about comparison.

---

4. I am aware that there is no objective method for determining, and agreeing on, what stands before our eyes. The same applies to the notion of 'empirical', which I use in this Introduction. These are issues I take up in *Western Rationality after Post-Colonialism*.

On the question of the Western gaze

It is argued, often with great vigour, that Westerners are singularly ill suited to understanding Africa. This has partly to do with the colonial legacy, which I discuss below. But it also has to do with a pervasive and powerful post-colonial argument: it is the very legacy of the Enlightenment that has brought about imperialism *and* a social theory that devalues the, particularly African, non-Western 'other'. Furthermore, racial thinking has permeated Western thought from the nineteenth century. Therefore, it is not just racism that blinds Westerners; it is the very theory they deploy to conceptualise society and politics. This is a powerful argument indeed and I want here to focus my attention on what it implies for the study of post-colonial politics in Africa.

Leaving aside the more general charge that Westerners are obsessed with the less palatable peculiarities of African politics and society, I want to discuss the issue of theory. It is widely alleged that the theories of politics that are applied to the study of the continent are either inappropriate or grossly distorting. What this means is that students of African politics unthinkingly apply Western theories without taking into account either the historical basis for these theories or the reasons why they may not be appropriate to the continent. This is partly true, as this book will demonstrate, but the question is whether this is a peculiarly anti-African bias.

Here arguments are less clear. Why would Western social scientists be more biased against Africa than about the rest of the non-Western world? The answer in plain language is threefold: racism, cultural superiority and colonialism. I deal with the third in the next section, so let me address the other two. It is a common assumption that, for historical reasons, Westerners are more racist, and more racist of Africans, than others. There is on the surface good ground for this belief but it runs into two serious difficulties. The first is that non-Westerners are demonstrably racist, particularly of Africans, as is made plain by long-held Indian and Chinese prejudice in this

anthropologists spoke the local languages, which is more than today's social scientists can say. The writers of exotic Africana may have been expiating more or less obscure original sins, which compelled them to travel into the 'darkness', but (like Conrad) they may have given account of a reality darker than even they realised.

Just because they were the products of their colonial times does not mean that there is no merit to their work. It is a lesser exercise to excoriate them for their lack of distance from their contemporary world than to read their work for our own contemporary world. It is a more rewarding exercise to make the effort of revisiting the issues that preoccupied them in order to assess the extent to which their efforts provide a sense of perspective from which we can essay our own analysis. The difficulty resides not in casting the anti-colonial stone but in determining the extent to which their work had value, both intrinsically and in terms of our own efforts to conceptualise politics in Africa. In this respect, there is much to be gained in reworking colonial archives and scholarship with an open mind. In any case, there ought to be nothing against doing so.

On the legitimacy of generalisation

I will not discuss here the question of generalisation per se, a topic to which I return in the Conclusion, but I will take up the critical issue of whether it is legitimate to generalise about contemporary Africa. The argument against such an enterprise is clear and straight-forward: Africa, a continent of fifty-three independent countries, is too varied and too complex to be encompassed in such broad sweep. And in many ways this is true, especially when trying to convey the specificities of such diversity. The question, however, does not hinge on the complexity of the continent but on the grounds for discussing it as a whole for analytical purposes. And here the issue is less simple.

It is customary, and no less sensible for it, to divide the continent into four distinct zones: north Africa, the Horn, sub-Saharan Africa and South Africa. Such divisions merely pay heed to the different histories, societies and cultures of these four areas and imply no hierarchy. They are simply a useful device for research. This book is about sub-Saharan Africa. But even here, there is a strong argument against generalisation. So what of it? The debate centres on two main issues: local societies are too disparate to make valid generalisations on their dynamics; diversity within each country is so great as to make cross-country comparisons untenable. These are two valid points and they do make clear the limits of generalisation.

The question here, however, is whether such local complexity and diversity invalidate comparison across sub-Saharan Africa any more than they do elsewhere. No one objects today to studies of European or South American politics, even if all recognise the enormous differences to be found between countries within these larger conglomerations. Nor is anyone denying that there are huge dissimilarities between the different regions of these individual countries. Why, then, should Africa be any different. To invalidate generalisation on the grounds of diversity is to refuse to compare. What matters is the nature of the generalisations undertaken.

The real question, therefore, is to justify the type and degree of generalisation that are deployed. Not all generalisations are appropriate, or even helpful, but some afford us a more refined understanding of local issues. A worthwhile generalisation, then, will engage the study of the local and bring relevance to bear on its analysis. The value of a generalisation is not best gauged in the abstract but in the study of how much sense it makes locally. If it provides perspective or if it helps cast a new light, then it has served its purpose. Otherwise, it is of limited interest. Generalisations are not right or wrong per se; they are merely another level of analysis of local empirical reality cast in a useful comparative framework.

The seven chapters that comprise the body of the book focus on what I consider to be the key moments and fundamental issues that mark human existence in contemporary Africa. The first three

– Being, Belonging and Believing – map out the core dimensions of life, the pillars of identity and sociability. The next two – Partaking and Striving – try to address the question of how individuals manage the political and economic opportunities as well as constraints with which they are confronted. The last two chapters – Surviving and Suffering – attempt to make concrete both the enormous difficulties Africans face in their daily lives and the extraordinary resources they deploy to overcome them.

Although these seven chapters can be read separately, there is a strong developmental thread to the way in which they have been written and linked. In their own way, they mirror the cycle of life as it is presently experienced in Africa. They also chart the incremental complexity of lives as they are lived, from the consolidation of social identity to the search for resources and status, all the while facing the pitfalls of a perilous, and often unforgiving, material existence. I hope that in this way the book will bring not just some analytical clarity but also a sense of the politics of ordinary lives in today's Africa. This would be but a small token of my admiration for the men and women I have met in a continent to which I have returned regularly since the early 1970s.

ONE

The politics of being

In this chapter I want to try to capture both the nature of the 'individual' and the politics of 'existence'. Although it may appear that such an approach is abstract, or vague, what I would like to do is very concrete. The aim here is to think about basic concepts, which we usually take for granted. We live in a world where, for instance, we do not often ponder the definition of the individual or spiritual foundations of existence. We study politics as though we could take for granted what it is about and how it works. This may well be convenient in the day-to-day business of explaining what our politicians are doing in our own countries, but it is limiting when we try to understand what is happening in settings very different from our own. It is indeed this very unreflective attitude that has led us to explain politics in Africa in terms that are all too often simplistic. If we are to think afresh, we must start at the beginning – that is, with what I call the politics of being.

It is customary in political science to construct analysis on the assumption that society is made of discrete units: individuals who have organised themselves to distribute and regulate power. This is a reasonable assumption but, on reflection, a very crude one. What in practice 'individual' and 'society' are, is not straightforward, and this is for two reasons. The first is that the actual definition of each depends on the relationship between the two: individuals are members of a particular society; societies are composed of particular individuals. The second is that, other than in strictly biological terms, the very notion of individual is problematic: human beings are contextually constructed. Nevertheless, even the best Africanist political science leaves untouched the question of how the tangible elements of people's 'existence' matter for the reality of what it means to be an 'individual'.

Right from the start, then, any approach to politics in Africa must tackle the question of what I call *being* − by which I mean the place and role of individuals within the environment in which they are born and live. The notion of being is not one that is designed to imply that this existential dimension is either unique to, or more significant in, Africa. It applies everywhere. Indeed, it would be useful, and I suspect enlightening, to take such an approach when discussing politics in the West as well. However, it is clear that it applies differently in different types of society and the key is to try to tease out the political implications of distinct ways of being. The intention here is to highlight areas that are common to all African societies, even if it is evident that there are vast, and vastly relevant, distinctions to be made between individuals within each society and between different communities.

I try to engage this issue by looking at three particular aspects of the question: *origin*, *identity* and *locality*. Although it may appear that these are self-evident 'givens', the founding blocks of any individual, this is not straightforwardly the case. Not only do these three concepts mean different things in separate settings but they are invested with different political meanings. Moreover, existing political theories approach them distinctly. And it is the political in which I am primarily interested. The point of looking at these three dimensions of the individual is not so much to provide a single definition of what they might mean in Africa − assuredly a fruitless quest − but to discuss the relevance they have both to the understanding and to the workings of politics at the local, regional and national levels. For this reason, I pay particular attention to the discourses attached to these terms and the political uses to which they have been put in post-colonial Africa.

One final caveat: the first two chapters are very closely connected. In some sense they cover the same ground but in complementary ways. They are here separated purely for analytical reasons. They address similar questions but come at them from different angles. The first tries to look at the identity of the person; the second at the nature of that person's place in society. However, there is little doubt in my mind that 'being' and 'belonging' are two sides of the same coin, as it were, and that it would be pointless to try to discuss one without the other. Indeed, what 'being' is perceived to be cannot be dissociated from what 'belonging' in practice is. Similarly, as should be obvious, the three categories below are also interlinked and overlapping.

ORIGIN

The literature on African politics pays very little attention to this question other than in terms of ethnicity. It is in this way directly continuous with the colonial vision of Africans, which built on the assumption that the continent's inhabitants were primarily 'tribal' and that origin mattered first and foremost because it helped identify the nature of such 'tribal' identity. I return below to the question of identity but I want here to show how that vision of Africans has not only privileged an approach in terms of ethnicity but has also led to the neglect of crucial issues, which matter greatly for politics. The importance of distinguishing between identity and origin lies in the ability it gives us to deploy a thicker analysis of issues that are central to human beings – in Africa as elsewhere. The first step, therefore, is to clarify what origin means.

I mean here to touch on two separate issues: one has to do with the question of location – the place of birth or, if birth occurred elsewhere, the location of the family origin; the second is concerned with the importance of the link to the actual geographical site. Let me explain. We are all born somewhere but the symbolic and practical relevance of that location varies greatly. As a general rule, a place of birth matters if it is connected to other factors which are relevant to identity. The strongest such factors are family (in its broadest sense), history or community relations. Indeed, unless the birthplace is in such way identified, it tends to be neglected. That much is common to us all. To take non-African examples, and in so far as one can generalise: the French have historically been especially concerned to have been born 'somewhere'; the Americans do not much care, even if they remember. The former value a sense of origin; the latter place more emphasis on who they are. The import of birth thus differs in these two Western societies.

In Africa, the places of birth and burial (the two being linked) matter greatly, fundamentally even, for a number of important religious, cultural and sociological reasons.[1] Contrary to what is commonly believed, the place of origin is less a marker of ethnic identity than it is a marker of community (the two are not synonymous, as I will discuss later). Among the many important dimensions of origin, I want to highlight three in particular: *land, ancestors* and *belief system*. They form the core of what I would call the constraints of origin – although they are not normally perceived as such: they are so central to the sense of identity as to be taken entirely for granted. They are also obviously intertwined, and to such an extent that it becomes difficult to talk of one without discussing the other. For the sake of exposition, I take them in turn.

Land is the physical site that marks origin. It is fundamental, and prior, in every sense since it delimits the actual physical boundaries of the location whence people come and it identifies the features that identify this world: mountains, rivers, forests, lakes, savannah, sea, desert, and so on. Often there is a direct connection between a

---

1. As is powerfully illustrated in Cohen and Odhiambo, 1992.

people's myth of origin and the physical landmarks of the land they now inhabit. Oral histories explain in some detail why it is that the group is, or has come to be, in the actual physical location it now occupies. The story as it is told usually provides an explanation of why there is an intimate, not to say symbiotic, relation between what the group is and the site that defines its geographical identity. Life began when the gods touched the top of the mountain or poured the water that made the river.

But land is more. It is the environment within which a people have learnt how to live and work. 'Traditional' occupations – grazing, fishing, cultivating, and so forth – are set within the context of the site. A group's various identities are derived from the relation it has had with the location and, even when they move, the members of that group continue to identify themselves as people of an area that is linked with particular occupations. This in itself may not matter greatly but it has a bearing on other aspects of identity and belonging. In Africa, occupation is frequently more important than ethnicity, as is obvious in the case of pastoralists. But it also matters in countries like Rwanda and Burundi where identity is derived as much from sociological as from ethnic factors – or rather, where the two cannot be dissociated. Elsewhere, there are profound and lasting issues having to do with the role of, for example, forests or sea, which continue to have an impact on how people see themselves and how they view their neighbours. Land, in short, is not just a physical attribute but is constitutive of what 'being' means – in the sense that it provides the context within which people define and organise themselves in socio-political terms. It also conditions the local political economy.

However, by far the most significant aspect of origin is the relation between the living and the dead – or the link to the *ancestors*. Of course, ancestors and land are intimately connected in the very real sense that the ancestors inhabit a concrete world that is identifiable within the geographical location from which the individual-within-the-group hails. Which is to say that the two cannot be dissociated artificially – for example, by offering an exchange of land or by relocating a particular group to another area, however economically attractive this may otherwise appear to be. The bond between land and ancestors is a given and may not be altered. It is the elemental reference point for the group, from which derive both belief and identity. To call it a reference point, however, is not to make it a causal determinant. People do not necessarily behave politically according to land and ancestors. It is the framework within which they identify themselves and it may, or may not, have political consequences, as we shall see.

The question of the ancestors, about which there is a large body of (mostly anthropological) work, is often misunderstood. The issue is not so much whether Africans 'believe' in the cult of the ancestors, as though this marked out their religion as somehow being more primitive. It is rather that the relation of group to land and the sense of origin are both rooted in the location where the ancestors are buried and propitiated. Nor is it a question of disputing the geographical position of such location – arguing for instance that more distant ancestors cannot possibly have been buried in this particular place. Rather it is that the link to the ancestors, wherever they are buried, is an integral part of the meaning of origin, and of the texture of identity, which cannot be disregarded. Therefore, there can be no complete sense of being that is not embodied in a physical place, which marks the link between the world of the living and the dead. Life itself is defined by that long chain. Today that chain may often be broken, in that individuals (youth, for instance) are now detached from their place of origin. This is not trivial, for them or for others; it has an impact on their sense of identity and on their own conception of their place in the world.

The relation between land and ancestors is, therefore, the very foundation of the *belief system*, or religion. Again, this is an element of African social life that has often been caricatured, not least by contemporary social scientists who have considered it a relic of outdated traditions. The key point here is not so much that African beliefs are rooted in the cult of ancestors, which is not an adequate way of translating what this means in practice. It is to try to explain how the belief system upon which ethical and socio-political values are erected draws intimately from the actual place of origin, the location and the roots of the self-acknowledged individual-within-the-community. This matters greatly for politics, in at least two important ways. One is that politics and politicians cannot be dissociated from their link to a concrete physical location, a place of origin to which they belong. The other is that the local remains central to the identity and action of all political actors, even if they operate primarily at the national level.

A great deal of what is seen merely as the parochialism of politics in Africa – including what seems to be an excessive partiality on the part of national politicians towards their home 'area' – cannot be adequately understood without reference to the meaning of origin. Of course, this is not to say that there is no corruption or that politicians do not abuse this aspect of the belief system, which they share with their constituents. It is to point out that any assessment of such abuse can only be made once it is understood what origin means. This varies according to groups and locations, and the actual details of the belief system are critical to a realistic understanding of these factors. What is not in question, however, is the relevance of such a dimension to political analysis. Here, as in many other areas, political scientists have comforted themselves in the idea that these questions were best left to anthropologists. They now need to realise that unless they address them squarely, they will be left without the means of determining the key reciprocal influences between the local and the national, which impinge on every aspect of political life in every African country.

IDENTITY

Of all the issues connected with the study of African societies, none has been more problematic than that of identity. It is in a very real sense the most basic question confronting the social scientist who tries to conceptualise which local factors matter for social and political behaviour. Accordingly, there is no shortage of work on this question, which I cannot summarise here. Instead, I want to suggest that this is very much an area in which the questions asked actually do determine the answers. Historically, the colonial mindset subsumed virtually all issues of identity under the vague rubric of tribalism. This did not just influence how colonial governments behaved, it also had a profound impact on the ways in which Africans instrumentalised their identity in the colonial and post-colonial context. Anthropologists, though they were often seen to comfort the colonial officials' equation of identity to tribe, were still likely to give a more refined account of how people viewed themselves. They were also more likely than officials to show that identity was contextual and adaptable. Nevertheless, they too frequently limited the range of possible interpretation.

I have shown elsewhere how the idea of a single concept of identity is misleading and why it is more useful to conceive of that notion in terms of overlapping circles of identity.[2] This means that in each instance we must try to analyse the historical and local context within which to identify those markers of distinctiveness that are more salient. Unfortunately, much Africanist political analysis continues to limit research to a small number of broad 'sociological' factors – such as ethnicity, religion and occupation – which are both too general and too limiting. Too general in that they may or may not be salient. Too limiting in that they presume that such are always the key markers of identity, when that may well not be the case. Research into identity ought to be guided more firmly by local knowledge resulting from the observation of what matters politically in the particular setting – bearing in mind that this will clearly change over time.

Questions of identity are directly linked to those of belonging, discussed below. Here I want to follow the gist of the previous

---

2. Chabal and Daloz, 1999: ch. 4. With reference to books written with Daloz 'I' implies co-authorship.

section and suggest that the most useful way of approaching this issue is to try to ascertain, in each given setting, what is and what is not negotiable. Let me hasten to add a key caveat: what is or is not negotiable is not immutable; it too changes over time, so that what we are doing here is to speak of the contemporary. As I explained above, matters of origin are not negotiable but, contrary to received wisdom on identity, most other markers are negotiable. And it is here that context-specific knowledge is required. For reasons having to do with their ubiquity in the literature, let me illustrate in more detail two broad areas of identity that are relevant to this discussion: *ethnicity* and *religion* − both of which are habitually taken to be non-negotiable when this is in fact not the case.

Although there is today a welcome renewal of interest in the question of *ethnicity*, which follows a long period when it was deemed to have been constructed, or even invented, by colonial rule, there is as yet insufficient attention paid to the fluidity of the concept. It is still used all too blithely as though its mere mention could ever be a sufficient explanation of political action. The distinction Lonsdale makes between ethnic morality and political tribalism has been helpful especially in the context of the author's detailed discussion of Kikuyu moral economy.[3] So is Hydén's remark that ethnicity is more social than cultural.[4] However, these are rare refinements of what remains a very crude and essentialising approach to the study of African identity. Moreover, the situation has been made worse by the huge, and ever growing, literature on conflict, which has often merely presumed that ethnicity was the key cause of violence.

Historically, ethnicity was a hybrid category, encompassing a range of social, cultural and economic markers. These were aggregated in different ways at different times. Not only was the notion of what it meant to belong to a particular ethnic group fluid but the criteria of appurtenance themselves could shift and evolve. Ethnicity was negotiable in many important ways: the genealogy of the group was

---

3. Lonsdale, 1992, 1994, 1995.
4. Hydén, 2006.

broad and encompassing, expanding and contracting as necessary; people could move in and out of ethnic groups; the geographical boundaries of the grouping were vague, with a roughly agreed core and many fraying edges; both the 'ideology' and the 'religion' of the group were susceptible to change, either because of external events or simply because of migration, disease, and so on. Finally, individual and kinship groups could change their ethnic identity in many different ways, since language in itself was not a restrictively defining standard of belonging.

Although colonial rule formalised and ossified what had hitherto been flexible congeries of fluid group affiliations, it did not obliterate pre-colonial processes of identification. If ethnic groups became (fairly) rigidly defined and classified, individuals continued to move across boundaries. What changed decisively, however, was the instrumentalisation of ethnicity as the chief characteristic of social identity. As the colonial order was organised along ethnic lines, political action followed suit. Ethnicity became the language by which colonial masters and subjects set down the political agenda and organised representation. Even where, as in the French colonies, colonial governments favoured politics on a regional or territorial basis, and combated mobilisation on strictly ethnic lines, the introduction of elections based on universal suffrage stimulated the political deployment of ethnic considerations.

The politicisation of ethnicity, or the universal development of political tribalism, was greatly exacerbated after independence. Many African politicians realised that electoral competition would further intensify ethnic rivalry, tension and violence but found it expedient to continue to use this form of mobilisation. At the same time, the massive expansion of a modern form of patrimonialism along these newly congealed ethnic lines led to a system in which both political and economic factors favoured the ever greater 'ethnicisation' of African life. The fact that it began to loom larger in post-colonial politics should not be taken as evidence that ethnicity had necessarily become more central to the identity of most people on the continent. Ethnicity became the ubiquitous political language but ordinary men and women continued to see themselves, and consider others, as complex and multilayered individuals, with whom they interacted on a large number of registers. If ethnicity has become the weapon of choice, both for politics and violence, it has almost never acquired the 'essentialised' significance that outsiders have tended to attribute.

The same goes for *religion*, at least for 'established' religion – by which I mean Christianity and Islam. Africa has long been seen, at least by Europeans and Arabs, as a terrain of choice, where indigenous beliefs would not resist the sweep of monotheistic religion – even if there is strong evidence that outside religious influence has not always been as strong as is commonly believed. The most thoroughly converted areas – the region bordering the Muslim north and east, as well as the eastern and southern settler colonies where Africans were most brutally deracinated – give the lie to the bulk of the continent, where conversion was both languid and functional. As many missionaries discovered in the nineteenth century, Africans converted out of convenience or interest – rarely out of conviction. Nor, much to the chagrin of the missionaries, did conversion imply the abandonment of Africans' own 'native' beliefs. African religions have always been highly adaptable and did not find it difficult to accommodate the strange dogma and rituals of the foreigners' creeds.

What is most remarkable about (established) religion, then, is that it was an intermittent and additional register of identity that neither displaced nor undermined those that harked back to the pre-colonial period. For most of the colonial period, the political relevance of religious divisions was vastly exaggerated. Even in northern Nigeria, today the scene of what seems to be bitter and violent confrontation, Christians and Muslims had been living and working side by side for generations. The clashes came later, after independence, when competition for resources within an increasingly frantic neo-patrimonial system encouraged rivalry and resentment, for which religion became a convenient vehicle. To some, it may today seem hard to fathom that Islam is anything other than fundamentalist but at least in Africa it has historically been highly syncretic. African Muslims have long practised a form of Islam that accommodates local religious beliefs and makes space for socio-cultural practices that are nowadays frowned upon. So it has been with Christians, even in circumstances where the European missionaries threatened fire and brimstone. And, where necessary, African prophets have set up their own Christian churches, adapting foreign religion to local beliefs.

There is today an unmistakable hardening of religious belief in Africa on both sides of the great divide. Some Muslims, particularly in West Africa, are pushing a highly partisan reformist agenda and have links with fundamentalists elsewhere. Conversely, the great Pentecostal wave is sweeping across the continent, as it is in Latin America, resulting in massive conversions to a narrow form of Christianity, which rejects local beliefs and provides a strong sense of identity for those who feel they have been cast aside. These are significant developments with clear political implications but they are neither as new nor as radical as they appear. First, there have been waves of Islamic reform in the past, which have had strong political impact (among others the nineteenth-century jihad movements). Similarly, the Zionist and Kimbanguist movements, among others, had considerable influence in some areas of colonial Africa for long periods, even if they are now much diminished. On the whole these various spiritual 'revolutions' did not result in new forms of identity within which religion had suddenly become non-negotiable. Much as might have been expected, religious zeal had to compromise with myriad other factors that make up what I call the 'politics of being'.

LOCALITY

Here, I want to bring together the strands from the previous two sections to show that questions of origin and identity come together in the notion of community, or locality. On the face of it, this is a fuzzy, catch-all, category, which covers a very large number of possible forms of grouping. I will explore in the next chapter the concrete manifestations of community life. I would like at this stage to delve into the question of how people identify themselves and live together in society, how they evolve within the group of people into which they are born and which stands at the centre of their social life. This is important in itself if we are to understand the nature of the relationship between individual and society, and thereby the political context within which people live. But it is also important because it needs to serve as a warning against the simplifications of Western political theories that are based on the primacy of the a-contextualised individual, with no regard to how the very concept of individual is problematic and simply cannot be taken for granted.

It has often been remarked that in Africa the communal and local dimensions prevail over that of the individual. However, that observation is rarely developed conceptually or analytically. If it is discussed at all, it is either relegated to the question of ethnicity – that is, the influence of what is assumed to be the key marker of individual identity – or it is seen as a leftover from traditions that are fast (even if, in fact, not so fast) disappearing. In both instances, the presumption is that such communal aspects are but staging posts in a universal process of human development that results in converging forms of individualisation. Such considerations as may be made about this communitarian aspect do not prevent standard political theory from operating on the premise that individuals are the building blocks of politics, in Africa as elsewhere. As a result, analysis is concerned primarily to identify the causes of individual action, which, it is imagined, can be ascertained by means of questionnaires or surveys canvassing individual opinions. The problem is not so much that such opinions are not valid but simply that they can only be interpreted usefully when they are set within a broader socio-cultural framework.

Although colonial anthropology gave a picture of Africa as being essentially communal in nature, its conception of what that meant was limited. First, it operated on the assumption that the tribal unit was crucial. Second, it fitted discussions of kinship, a mainstay of classical anthropology, into that ethnic mould. Third, it gave very little attention to the dynamics of this supposedly tribal existence, and in particular to the ways in which traditions might have been modified by colonial rule or by other outside influences. Anthropologists, it seemed, had nothing to teach those political scientists who came in the 1960s to study the politics of modernisation in the newly independent African countries. Recent anthropological work, however, has been much more enlightening and I want to revisit the question of the relevance of locality to politics by focusing attention on those aspects of the relationship between 'community' and 'individual' I see as most relevant: *gender, age* and *authority*.

In contemporary Africa, *gender* issues are complex and many of those who discuss them have their own agenda. For instance, much has been made of the fact that in some countries the proportion of women MPs has grown considerably or that there are today many prominent women politicians. This is true as far as it goes but how deeply it affects actual politics on the ground is debatable – and certainly needs further research. The use of gender quotas may not be very effective at changing the nature of political participation. On the other side, numerous NGOs have pointed to the precarious conditions endured by women who are subjected to the pressures, constraints and even violence of 'tradition'. Many deplore the lack of opportunity and education for women and all condemn female genital mutilation. There is plenty of evidence to sustain these campaigns. However, I am more concerned here to touch on the place of women as individuals-within-the-community and to try to assess the extent to which the current condition of women is (merely) a reflection of patriarchy or whether it arises out of a complex combination of 'traditional' and 'modern' factors. How does the division between men and women affect politics?

If, as I have argued, questions of origin and identity are crucial, then it is clear that gender cannot be dissociated from the socio-cultural considerations that link these two factors. Women are not just 'females'; they come from particular places and they share most circles of identity with males from their community of origin. This means, among other factors, that their female identity is partly determined by the 'traditions' of that community, regardless of whether they live in their place of origin, partly by the effects of that community's moral and ethical standards and partly by their place in the local political economy. It is difficult, therefore, to generalise about women in Africa since many of these factors are contextually distinct. However, what is clear is that, in most societies, women inhabit a clearly delineated space with its own rules regarding social, economic and political activities. If women often are successful economic actors, they rarely engage directly in open politics and even more rarely stand for elected local office. Even where quotas are introduced, women are still subject to community constraints and, for example, rarely enter politics against the wishes of the significant male kin members.

The key point here is that in this respect, as in many others, it is important to stress the local aspects of female identity. Women and men are not autonomous sexualised individuals but female and male members of specific groupings, the ethos and values of which impinge strongly on their identity. Within such a context, the ways in which one behaves and belongs as a woman is inscribed in a long history. Changes both in the definition of female/male identity and in the ways 'traditions' affect political behaviour are slow and incremental. For this reason, it is necessary to pay particular attention to what are sometimes called the informal aspects of political roles and political action. Even the most ostensibly 'modern' politicians, including women, are in effect bound by ethical codes that are only fully intelligible if interpreted against the norms and values of particular localities. Much of what passes for corrupt or partisan action may also need to be explained in communal terms.[5] Of course,

---

5. Even if it cannot be denied that communal excesses cover a variety of sins, many of which have nothing to do with 'tradition' and boil down to sheer greed.

this does not mean that such norms and codes are to be condoned; simply that they need to be understood in their local context.

Similarly, *age* plays an important role in one's social position within a community. It is significant not just in terms of social hierarchy and political prominence – both of which are undeniably crucial – but also in terms of one's own identity. However irrelevant it may seem in the era of fast modernity and sweeping globalisation, the notion of age group continues to have strong resonance in everyday life. Age is not merely a numerical marker in a continuous chronological series. Human beings are defined in part by their age and their position within the relevant age grouping. Even where rites of initiation no longer take place or carry much less conviction, the notion that male and female members of a community belong to a particular age group is of significance. Individuals are not only the sons and daughters of particular parents – and here, too, the term 'parent' can cover a variety of familial members – they are also the products of a particular groups as defined by the norms of age aggregation that are current in that particular locality. To say this is not to imply that age is determinant. It is not. But it may become salient, or politically relevant, in certain circumstances.

For instance, we know that in the Liberian conflict the violence was often organised and carried out according to 'rules' that derived from age-group politics.[6] Both the 'ideology' and 'practice' of the violence could be related to, though obviously not 'explained' by, the disciplining and marshalling of brutality along such 'traditional' lines. Similarly, many of the violent groupings that used child soldiers to carry out atrocities during civil conflicts in Africa imposed their will by forcing young people to break the 'taboos' associated with age in their own community. By compelling these children to degrade, humiliate, mutilate and kill elders or parents, the warmongers cast them out of their community, to which they could never return – at least not without undergoing ceremonies of reintegration. This is

---

6. Ellis, 1999.

not an irrelevant factor in the understanding of the genealogy and pathology of conflicts that have afflicted vast swathes of the continent and devastated generations of Africans.

In another register, it is essential to acknowledge the role of age in relations between politicians both within individual countries and across borders. It is widely acknowledged by Africanists that references to senior statesmen in terms that denote the experience, wisdom and equanimity associated with age are ubiquitous. Yet too little attention is paid by political scientists to the implications of such discourse for actual political action. Two examples will illustrate this point. Military takeovers by younger officers or even politicians often require the symbolic, sometimes physical, elimination of their elder politicians – as though they cannot aspire to legitimacy so long as their seniors are still active, or alive. And indeed, more often than not, a key reason why legitimacy is denied has to do with this aggression against age. Finally, it has been argued by some that one of the reasons Thabo Mbeki has never applied real pressure on Robert Mugabe was because he could not bring himself to exercise the leverage his country's stature would command upon someone who was a nationalist father figure, or elder. Whether true or not, the fact that this is mentioned speaks to the relevance of the attributes of age.

The issue of age is intimately connected with that of *authority*, which is the last aspect of locality I want to stress in this chapter. Political science is concerned with the exercise of power, which all too often is unthinkingly assimilated to authority. However, the two are different in ways that matter. Power can be approached from a variety of different angles but it essentially entails the ability to force others to comply; by coercion if necessary. Authority implies a position of trust, competence and wisdom that confers upon those who are endowed with it the force of persuasion, rather than coercion. One can exercise power without authority but one cannot have authority without being acknowledged by others to be worthy of it.

Of course, in long-established and institutionalised political systems power and authority very largely overlap, though they are never
equivalent. In African countries, on the other hand, the two are
quite clearly separate, even if some politicians are able to combine
their attributes successfully. Not only must authority and power
be conceptualised separately, they must also be placed in their appropriate context. Comparative politics has very little to say on the
matter save for the trivial, though not wholly untrue, remark that
the former belongs to the realm of 'tradition' whereas the latter is
of the 'modern'. Yet this only confuses the issue because it confines
it to a simplistic dichotomy that does not reflect reality and, more
significantly, fails to come to terms with the ways in which 'tradition'
and 'modernity', formal and informal, actually overlap or coexist.

Issues of authority have been acute since the colonial period
because the imperial powers contrived to rearrange 'native' political
structures to their best convenience. This meant collaborating with
established chiefs in some instances and appointing so-called colonial
chiefs in other cases. The result was the creation of a political
system in which power and authority became dissociated. Even
legitimate 'traditional' leaders, recognised as such by the population, were discredited when it became obvious they had to become
colonial auxiliaries. Their authority was not necessarily in doubt but
it became clear that authority without colonial endorsement meant
powerlessness. As for 'colonial' chiefs, they never acquired legitimate
authority but they could sometimes exercise enormous power. The
post-colonial transition confused matters even more since in most
cases it amounted to a nationalist 'coup' by a generation of politicians
that lacked either age or 'traditional' authority but who wielded
virtually untrammelled power. Since then, not only have authority
and power grown further apart but new questions have arisen about
the legitimacy of politicians, and even of politics *tout court*.

Since independence, politicians have sought, with uneven success,
to combine power with authority. If in the early days of the postcolony it seemed they had managed either to obliterate or usurp

'traditional' authority, it became apparent during the one-party period that this was not the case. Not only did 'traditional' kings, chiefs and spirit mediums continue to exercise authority, but the 'modern' politicians themselves began to feel the need to acquire 'traditional' authority. This was not just for the reasons adduced by political scientists: that is, as an instrumental means of buttressing their legitimacy. It was also, and perhaps more importantly, because politicians remained part of their grouping of origin as defined above and their own identity rested in part on their ability to propitiate the keepers of their locality. In other words, these politicians themselves realised that their 'modern' roles did not really address the demands of the 'traditional' world to which they also belonged and in respect of which they defined themselves as individuals. As we shall see later, the influence of the community is perhaps most graphically demonstrated by the impact of witchcraft upon national politicians, who thus remain susceptible to local pressure.

To conclude, the concept of the *politics of being* is an attempt to focus attention on issues of identity and locality that are usually neglected or, worse, taken for granted. Because most political theories of Africa rehearse the same arguments about the primacy of certain forms of identification, especially ethnicity, they overlook other, arguably more important, questions concerning the meanings of the individual, the import of origin, the significance of age and the nature of authority. These markers of identity, which are particularly relevant in Africa today, need to be studied in their local and historical context. They all have distinct influence on the discourses and connotations of politics as well as on the complex ways in which power is exercised. They are also characteristics that filter the sense given to political issues and map out the texture of political opinion.[7]

---

7. Lest it be thought that these are areas of research that historians and social scientists cannot realistically manage, I would point to an excellent book touching on the importance of 'tradition' in the definition of legal property in Africa. See Berry, 2001.

TWO

The politics of belonging

If the previous chapter sought to discuss in somewhat Western terms what the meaning of individual existence is, this chapter tries to refine some of the concepts used by concentrating on the actual lived-through notion of belonging. What was Western about the approach in Chapter 1 was the attempt to define the individual and explain its main markers of identity, as though these were concretely distinct 'objects' that could be offered for analysis as such, unmediated. However, what makes African social relations what they are is the fact that individuals conceive of themselves in terms of the multiple and multifaceted relations which link them with others within ever-expanding and overlapping concentric spheres of identity. In practice, therefore, it is misleading to conceive of persons merely as individuals, as in the Western contemporary meaning of the term, and to consider individuals as the sole 'building blocs' of society. We should instead make the effort of reading the person in terms of the relations that have come to define its social position within a given historical, social, cultural and geographical space.

The purpose of this chapter is not so much to give an 'anthropological' account of the person in Africa, though I will make ample use of the insights provided by that discipline, as it is to explore some of the key issues in what I call the *politics of belonging*. What does this mean? Part of what we are as persons is defined by where we belong and what such belonging entails concretely. The politics of belonging, it should be made clear at the outset, is in no way a specific 'African' way of existing – as though only people from that part of the world were enmeshed in considerations of this nature. Far from it: in Africa as elsewhere one belongs but one belongs in different ways. I am interested here in trying to grapple with the actual dimensions of belonging that have noticeable political significance – by which I mean those that have had a clear influence on politics since independence.

As before, it is plain that this question has been neglected by political scientists, who have either ignored such factors or considered them as 'primordial', 'traditional' or ascriptive: attributes of ethnic identities or relics from a distant past and of diminishing relevance. Yet, most current analysis of African economic and socio-political issues is now having to come to terms with the consequences of the politics of belonging, if only because it has seemingly fuelled numerous conflicts, some ominously violent, of which Sierra Leone, Rwanda or Côte d'Ivoire may be seen as paradigmatic. There is presently a huge debate in Africa about rising hostility between 'natives' and 'strangers', or, in current francophone parlance, *autochthony* against *allochthony* – a debate to which I shall return in this and other chapters.[1] For now, I shall merely point out that this debate echoes that which took place during the colonial period, when the imperial powers sought to outline the boundaries of recognisable 'groupings' into which they could place their colonial subjects. Interestingly enough, their view was the opposite of that which prevails today in Africa: the 'outsider' was often imbued with greater qualities of work, strength and reliability than the more indolent native.

---

1. For the sake of simplicity of usage, and despite its disagreeable connotation, I shall use 'native' – and in the rest of the book without inverted commas – instead of autochthon, which is not yet commonly used in English, unlike in, say, French or Dutch. See Geschiere, 2008.

I try to tease out the politics of belonging from three different angles: that is, in terms of *kin*, *reciprocity* and *stranger*. I make no pretence here to use these concepts in classical anthropological fashion. Even less do I claim to give account of the anthropological material that is relevant to the discussion. My interest is not in definition as such but in the unpacking of the discourses underlying these generally agreed notions and in the assessment of their relevance to acutely political questions in contemporary Africa. What matters more is how the people concerned consider these three aspects of their lives and why they think they matter for politics.

The first and last sections will broach the question of kin and stranger, or in other words those who are, in Western terms, seen as relatives and those who are seen as foreigners. The second will touch on one of the key aspects of the difference between the two, reciprocity, and will discuss how this matters for the understanding of post-colonial politics in Africa. Again, there is plainly significant overlap between these three parts but I distinguish them analytically so as to facilitate discussion of their relevance to political theories of Africa.

KIN

The standard approach to questions of kinship in Africanist political science is to consider them either from the angle of ethnic identity or in terms of the 'weight', or burden, of relatives. The first stresses that individuals are related to members of their ethnic group in ways that are based on 'tradition' and precedence. This means that political behaviour is inflected by ethnic politics and more generally by relations of honour and debt, which have priority over other forms of social or professional relations. The second indicates that relatives in Africa are more often than not an encumbrance to the individual, who is seen thus to be impaired in his/her personal, professional or political activities. The limits of such approaches are two: one is that they confine discussion of kinship to the ethnic realm; the other is that they view these relations normatively – as being deleterious to the individualisation of the person *and* the involvement of individuals in the modernisation of their society, politics and economy. In other words, questions of kinship are presented in essentialist terms or, instrumentally, as being *ipso facto* antithetical to progress, whatever that may mean.

Therefore, what is missing is an appreciation of the nature of kinship in dynamic, rather than static, terms and of the 'modern', rather than 'traditional', political implications of such bonds. Following on from the discussion in Chapter 1, I focus here on two key aspects of kinship: *association* and *obligation*. These do not in any way exhaust the question but merely centre attention on two important features that are politically significant. Kin relations cut across stratification or hierarchy and thus link rich with poor, powerful with powerless, and urban with rural. Hence, they impinge on socio-political relations in ways that are rarely conceptualised in Africanist political science – where the variables used are limited to the standard sociological categories of ethnicity, region, religion, profession, class, profession, and so on. The key question here is not so much whether kinship trumps these as how they intersect in both the formal ('modern') and informal ('traditional') sectors.

The most useful way of approaching kinship in political analysis is to consider it as a vast *association* of people, connected to many other associations, or networks, at both local and translocal levels. Although in strictly technical terms kinship relates to closely related family and clan members as linked by marriage, what I mean here is broader in that it covers the concatenation of circles of relations that matter concretely to ordinary life. These, as we have seen, include the ancestors and, more generally, the dead. They are, however, bound by a connection to land, or locality, in ways that are always compelling. Whether matri- or patrilineal, kinship bonds do not only relate to individuals but to persons within clearly delineated networks and geographies. The bond that binds those who have left their area of origin is thus double: it concerns family and clan relations who have a claim on one's social identity *and* other individuals beyond this immediate circle who are linked by virtue of local proximity. One's responsibilities as an individual are in this way the mirror image of those features that contribute to one's identity as a human being.

Or, to put it another way, since the attributes of the person are inherently linked to the identity of the locality, one is only 'human' in so far as one is part of a kin network. It is for this reason that those who break from that bond or are cast away become non-persons, socially 'dead' as it were. This explains why the consequences of the collapse of the community is to create congeries of individuals who do not belong, in the most profound sense, and who must find other groupings in order to regain their 'humanity'. Where economic hardship destroys communities, those who are thrown out readily seek identity in religious groups, of which the Pentecostal churches are the most successful. Where violence tears out young people from their kinship associations, the company of killers often becomes the only relevant community to which they can belong – and which in turn defines who they are. They can only ever hope to regain their humanity if cleansed by the actual community of origin.

What is most significant about kinship, therefore, is not the (negative) burdens or (positive) opportunities it implies, which are real enough, but the ways in which it contributes to a sense of socially meaningful belonging. It must thus be conceptualised as that part of identity which confers value, legitimacy or merit to political action. If identity is largely communal, then politics itself must perforce reflect a collective dimension. It is not, as is usually advanced by political science, merely the agglomeration of individual actions. So, politics is not just about power, the ability to induce others to do what one wants; it is also the display of a collective 'virtue', which manifests the identity and qualities of the kin association in question. Politicians and followers, rulers and ruled, are all inextricably linked in a relation of unequal dependence, which I explore later, by which they relate to each other within the framework of the extended kin network(s) to which they belong.

The pursuit and display of virtue in this sense require a pro-
pitiation of the values of the association, which is channelled
by means of a system of *obligations*. I discuss below the critical
notion of reciprocity. Here I want to explain how obligations are
in effect the currency of the association, the value system upon
which it rests. In Western political theory the term 'obligation'
has acquired a fairly narrow instrumental meaning, which does
not convey what is involved here. Within a network, an obligation
defines how individuals relate to each other as human beings, and
not just what is expected of them by way of political transactions.
The web of obligations that link people is densest at the core of
the kinship association and more diffuse at its periphery. Obligations from different networks intersect. Nevertheless, there is no
clear and absolute division between the realms of obligation and
non-obligation: the very texture of social relations is woven from
ties of obligation, some of which are more compelling than others
in kinship terms.

What an obligation in practice means is an integral part of what
belonging is; the one goes with the other. One is a person, one
belongs, one is part of a community, *in so far* as one is integrated in
a complex system of authority, deference and participation, which
forms the backbone of the intersecting spheres of identity that matter
for life in that given society. The idea that an individual could live
utterly detached from any community is not one that finds favour,
or is even meaningful, in Africa – as is made clear by the pejorative
reputation such individuals inevitably acquire. Therefore, the question
is not whether to be party to a system of obligations or not but how
to manage one's place within such a system. To have no obligation is
not to belong; it is not to be fully and socially human. Obligations,
therefore, are not seen – as the Western concept seems to imply – as
impositions, claims on one's otherwise better used time and energy,
but as a means of sustaining one's place in a network of belonging:
that most vital attribute of humanity, sociability and, ultimately,
being-in-the-world.

The range of obligations is vast and comprises innumerable local variations. However, there are types of obligations that are found everywhere. These are tied to matters of origin, age, gender and beliefs. Perhaps the most fundamental obligation has to do with burial – a process that is critical to the public good since it establishes the vital link between the living and the dead. Burial is important not just because it is a key element in the cycle of life but also because it makes manifest and keeps alive the concrete link between the individual, the community and the land with which it is identified. It is thus the core of individual and collective identity, which defines the relationship between the person and the group, or network. A properly executed burial reinforces the collective sense of belonging, without which the person is not fully human and the community is not fully complete.

Lest it be thought that these considerations are either too abstract or too static, it is well to consider the political implications of kinship, as defined above. In so far as association and obligation determine the nature of both personal identity and of the social relations between those who are part of this form of relation, they also influence every aspect of the political process. Let me give two illustrations.

First, the understanding of what politics means is filtered through the system of values, of collective virtue and of the notion of public good, which is implied in kinship. What is right is what sustains this virtue, of which the main aspect is that the political space is occupied by a large number of (overlapping and interconnected) networks of obligations. In this context, it is apparent that the premise of a democratic dispensation – the utter and total equivalence between all individuals, or citizens – is difficult to integrate into the existing system of obligations. It can also be seen that multiparty elections are not immediately congruent with the underlying social framework of politics.

Second, the legitimacy of those who are in politics is predicated upon their meeting the obligations for which they have responsibility within the associations to which they belong. Even if politicians acquire other, more national and more universal, attributes within the country, they cannot be exempt from the requirements of the local public good. Put in cruder terms, it is simply not possible to opt out of one's community and to continue to belong – that is, effectively, and from the standpoint of that locality, to be fully human. This implies, with precious little ambiguity, that political action remains tributary to the norms of virtue that are attached to, and defined by, the associations of origin. Of course, it is the politician's challenge to fashion political space above and beyond such worlds of kinship but the weight of local obligations does not thereby diminish.

RECIPROCITY

In day-to-day socio-economic and political life, kinship translates into structures of reciprocity, which govern interpersonal and intra-communal relations. Wherever the boundaries of the network lie – and it is crucial to remember that these are always fluid and porous – they delineate the space within which obligations are inserted into schemes of reciprocity. Reciprocity is a broad concept, which needs refining in its local context. It also has different meanings in different disciplines. Here again, I shall draw on anthropology, particularly on the literature about gift and gift giving, which is at the basis of all forms of reciprocity. Among others, this material touches on the difference between gift and commodity, which anthropologists have discussed in respect of what appear to be radically distinct forms of economic intercourse. These are all interesting questions that are relevant to this discussion but my concern here is more specifically with those aspects of reciprocity that are most relevant to the politics of post-colonial Africa.

Current political theories of Africa consider reciprocity a 'traditional' aspect of society, one that is both antiquated and inimical to the 'modern' kind of politics an independent and forward-looking Africa requires. In this view, reciprocity is a drag on the transition towards the individual-based organisation of economics and politics that is seen to be the precondition of development and modernisation. Whether, or how, this is so is not my primary concern here since what I seek to understand is how reciprocity operates and how it colours the political realm. To that end I build on the notions of association, legitimacy and obligation discussed above. I look successively at the nature of (political) *exchange*, the meanings of (political) *representation* and the byways of (political) *accountability*. That is, I start from the premise that the politics of reciprocity are logical, coherent and legitimate – even if they have often been instrumentalised by politicians bent on taking, retaining and even abusing power.

In a system of identity-based reciprocity, there are well-established rules of *exchange*. These regulate the reciprocal obligations of different groups and individuals within networks. They also define the nature of political power. Two aspects of this type of exchange matter for politics: the tangible and the symbolic – the respective aspects of which overlap. It is not just a question of leaders acting as Big Men – that is, redistributing to their clients what they acquire by dint of their holding office or exercising power – although that is clearly at the heart of the material embodiment of exchange. It is also a matter of combining the material and symbolic in ways that satisfy the expectations of reciprocity held by both sides. In order to understand relations of exchange of that type, it is necessary to make sense of the two aspects, not just the more obviously visible and concrete one.

Such relations of exchange are unequal, based as they are on a clear reality of power (though not always authority, as we have seen): rulers expect to rule. Nevertheless, perhaps the most common blind spot among Africanist political scientists is the assumption that African leaders are merely corrupt dictators because they are not elected, or not elected properly, and because they ostensibly abuse their office. It is not so simple. What matters for members of the networks is less how politicians come to hold office and with what probity they occupy it than how they discharge their obligations under existing systems of reciprocity. Although some politicians do become tyrants, and thus break the relations of reciprocity that bind them to the networks that may have helped bring them to office, they rarely cut themselves off entirely from their community. And in this way they still remain beholden to the constraints of belonging that continue to govern their commitment to reciprocity whilst in office.

What this means is that the mechanisms of exchange continue to matter for politics, even when the legitimacy of the politicians in question has been seriously dented. With few exceptions, African rulers are unable to rule by fear or terror alone, not just because they rarely possess sufficient means of coercion but, more importantly, because they cannot afford to be deprived of their identity. They, too, will eventually have to be buried 'at home'. Or, to put it another way, there are two different types of legitimacy: the national and the local, each of which is governed by different rules. Even when politicians lose national legitimacy, they seek to retain local legitimacy. Whilst their standing as national politician depends intimately on combining the two types of legitimacy successfully, their political and even physical survival hinges on their submitting to the rules of local reciprocity. This is one of the factors that explain why spectacularly unsuccessful national politicians sometimes manage to make an unlikely comeback. This patrimonial quality, rather than merely abuse of power, is often the key to the longevity of politicians. On the other hand, politicians who are bereft of local legitimacy are finished politically since they have lost their key constituency.

The question of the legitimacy of politicians, therefore, is intimately connected to that of political *representation*. This is certainly a topic favoured by political scientists and there is a fair amount of work geared to understanding the basis of political legitimacy in post-colonial Africa. Here, it has been common to make a distinction between 'traditional' and 'modern' representation – the former being that which is embodied by the 'chiefs', or other 'traditional authorities'; the latter that which is sanctioned by elections. Part of the reason for such a distinction is historical in that the anti-colonial activists, who took power at independence, conceptualised the situation in this way: they were the 'modernists'. Another reason is that a similar dichotomy is to be found in political theory, where the difference marks what is supposed to lie at the heart of the process of modernisation. However, this is not a very useful distinction both because the situation is much more complex and because it distorts the analysis of the realities of representation in the African context.

It is more profitable to conceive of representation as comprising several, equally important, aspects – some 'modern' and some 'traditional' – all of which operating within this context of reciprocity. The first is conventional: the politician must represent the interests of the 'formal' constituency from which (s)he is elected. This requires ensuring that local demands are met in the competitive context of national politics. The second has to do with representing in the sense of belonging to: the politician is required to be a proper constituent member of the group as it defines itself. This means the representative has to possess the identity markers (e.g. ethnicity, religion) of the grouping. The third is concerned with representation being the embodiment of the virtue of the community of origin. Here the person is expected visibly to display those (entrepreneurial, martial, spiritual, etc.) qualities that are believed by the group concerned to matter most in material and symbolic terms. The last is less tangible but no less significant in that it touches on representation as the aspiration of the community: not what the grouping is but what it would like to think it is. In this respect, the representative must evidence those ambitions (e.g. wealth, fame, power) that best demonstrate the group's marks of honour, however delusional they appear to outsiders.

Again, it is immediately apparent that these forms of representation are not necessarily compatible and that they are well-nigh impossible to achieve in *toto*: hence the great frustration, and perennial contradictions, at the heart of the contemporary politics of representation in today's Africa. It is analytically self-defeating to consider all but the first aspect of representation as leftovers from slowly disappearing 'traditions', which are or ought to be irrelevant to the politics of modernising states. The reality is that they all matter, admittedly in unequal measure and in different ways, according to circumstances. They embody distinct types of reciprocity between politicians and populace, rulers and ruled, representatives and represented. They form the bonds of reciprocity that characterise the links between local and national politics.

Equally, it serves little purpose to classify them, rigidly, as either 'traditional' or 'modern' – they are both; just as it is pointless to devise schemes of political restructuring (for 'good governance', for example) that ignore these aspects. The more difficult task is to try to identify how these different levels operate and with what consequences they interact. Perhaps the best way to conceptualise political representation in such settings would be to conceive of it as a multidimensional system of reciprocity in which all those aspects matter simultaneously but with constantly varying energy depending on the historical, social and economic context within which politics is being played out. How they play out at any particular time is a question for local research.

In this respect, most Africanist political science discussions of legitimacy and representation fail to consider, even less allow for, these other, supposedly 'traditional', dimensions of the political edifice. They prefer instead to view success in such registers simply as the manipulation by political elites of 'traditional' factors. This is true only in a shallow sense since it entirely fails to come to terms with the fact that such factors are as essential to the representative as they are to the represented – for reasons having to do with the attributes of personhood, identity and belonging discussed above. Whilst it is undoubtedly the case that some African politicians (like Mobutu, Amin or Mugabe) placed themselves beyond the pale, as it were, most of those who have been seen merely as petty despots (like Kenyatta, Houphouët Boigny) continued to be endowed with (admittedly varying) qualities of representation long after they had exhausted the vital energy of 'virtue'.

The last aspect of reciprocity I want to highlight here is *accountability*. This, too, is a well-trodden topic in political theory, central as it is to all discussions of modern liberal political systems. The issue here, as it is of representation, lies with the multiplicity of meanings such a concept covers. To restrict its scope to the generally accepted realm of elections would be to limit the analysis of African politics to its virtual shadow. Not just because elections on the continent are problematic in terms of procedure, execution and transparency but also because they are but a small part of the process that matters politically. Although formal electoral accountability matters more now than it did a couple of decades ago, it matters only in some, and not necessarily the most meaningful, ways. To put it another way, politicians elected in multiparty dispensation are frequently considered by the population as being no more accountable than those elected in one-party systems or even, sometimes, those who have not been elected at all. Elections rarely equate directly with accountability. This is a conundrum Africanist political analysts must tackle, not evade.

The reason for this is that accountability should be conceptualised in terms of its two components: the person who is deemed to be accountable and the process by which accountability is measured.

The first is best seen within the context of belonging, legitimacy and representation discussed above – in its manifold dimensions. Politicians, as well as all those who have responsibility of authority within a local grouping (which obviously include numerous so-called 'traditional' authorities, medium spirits, etc.), are expected to be accountable in distinct fashions. To illustrate such differences in stark form, MPs should deliver resources to the community, chiefs should ensure rain falls and witch doctors should deal with the dark side of witchcraft. The measure of their accountability is tied to their perceived function – how that function is in practice political is a matter for research.

The second concerns the process of accountability, which also varies according to context. Those who have political responsibility are expected to submit to different forms of accountability if they are to retain legitimacy. On occasion, elected officials are endowed with a large number of representative qualities, both 'modern' and 'traditional', and they are thus legitimate in several different ways. Here, accountability may be encompassed within the electoral process, which can then be seen as the consecration of such multifaceted legitimacy. But such cases are rare. Most often there are a number of different forms of representation, formal and informal, by which people expect to be heard and to have influence. Here, the processes of accountability can be markedly different and need to be studied accordingly, with no prior agenda against 'tradition'.

What accountability is, therefore, cannot be decreed *a priori*, according to some given political theory which may apply in the West. It needs to be uncovered in its local context, and that context is always one of reciprocity – which is, of course, what accountability means in the first place. Given the nature of the state in Africa, where the formal and informal overlap to such a degree, even the understanding of 'modern' politics – parties, elections, parliaments, governments, governance, policies, and so on – requires an appreciation of informal accountability. I have explained elsewhere how this process of accountability hinges on the expectations of those who are represented.[2] In some instances, it will be assumed that the political elites enable their constituency privileged access to the resources of the state. In others, it will be expected that the proceeds from oil exports will be lavished in a particular region. In yet other settings, it might involve granting a minority group parity within a particular political dispensation.

The point here is simply that in a context where accountability is endowed with such different meanings and where it is enforced in so many different ways, the basis upon which it is to be explained

2. Chabal and Daloz, 1999: Part 1.

has to derive from an understanding of the nature and scope of reciprocity between different political actors – high and low. Similarly,
it is essential to pay attention to the informal processes of accountability, which are always operative in Africa and which frequently
have more traction on politics than the more elaborate and visible
formal electoral mechanisms. Two examples will serve as illustration.
Politicians who feel the need to enhance their 'traditional' legitimacy
– say, by acquiring a chiefly title – will necessarily have to respect
the forms of accountability that this entails. On the other hand,
national politicians who appear to their locality of origin to be
insufficiently accountable – meaning not responsive enough to local
demands – may well be forced to account by means of accusations
of witchcraft – accusations that can only be removed by restoring
the expected reciprocity.

STRANGER

The politics of belonging raises the question of the politics of non-
belonging, which has become acute in Africa today. It translates into
severe competition for resources and often degenerates into conflict.
Moreover, multiparty elections have brought to the surface a number
of issues related to origin, identity and locality that affect politics
in almost every country on the continent. Finally, there are now
increasingly severe problems of land ownership and of what might
be called cultural hegemony at the local level, which have raised the
levels of tension between peoples who may have lived together for
generations. The issue of who is a 'native' (autochthon) and who
is a 'stranger' (allochthon) is now at the centre of the struggle for
power at both local and national levels – and this at a time when
it was presumed that such parochial differences would reduce with
modernisation.

Africanist political scientists are often at a loss here, unsure of
what to make of what seem arcane debates about ascriptive attributes
they don't know well and whose relevance they find difficult to

ascertain. Although there is a well-established literature in the Western social sciences about the 'stranger' (or the 'other'), much of it having to do with psychological factors, such theories seem irrelevant to the African case, where issues are more complex. Because the notion of stranger is multi-stranded and situational, it is difficult to identify clearly who belongs to this category. Simple concepts such as foreign origin or migrant do not fit the African case well since it is notoriously the case that Africans have moved and continue to move incessantly between locations. Other definitions encompassing language, ethnicity or religion again largely fail to provide sufficiently plausible explanations for some of the present conflicts.

It is best to start to start from the observation that the concept of belonging is both contextual and historical – meaning thereby that it is not fixed, enshrined in some legal document to which jurists could refer in order to adjudicate. It is both changing and contingent. The thrust of the first two chapters of this book has been to suggest how delicate it is to tease out the actual meaning of origin, identity and belonging. Indeed, it is not possible precisely to determine what these are in the abstract; only the thick description of the particulars makes it possible to appreciate what they convey and then only at a given period in history. There is in this way no shortcut to local research. All I can do here is to point to the general questions raised by the attempt to understand the notion of stranger contextually. The generalisations concern the questions, not the answers – which are only valid in local terms.

The reasons why the issue of strangers has become more serious recently are many but a few stand out. First, economic hardship in a context of limited development has created conditions of increasing competition and growing poverty – conditions which, as everywhere else in the world, trigger xenophobic attacks on those deemed to be the 'outsiders' who are robbing the locals of opportunities or resources. Second, the transition from single- to multiparty political systems, with their attendant electoral contests, in a context where access to formal power remains the most direct route to national resources, has led to increasingly bitter political contests. Third, the growing impact of an apparently unstoppable process of globalisation, both economic and cultural, has provoked strong local reactions, which are often expressed through real or imagined cultural nationalisms – thus focusing attention upon what are supposed to be the attributes of local culture. Fourth, growing diasporas often support such imagined nationalism. Therefore, I propose to get at the question of who a stranger is from these three different angles: *economic, political and cultural.*

From the *economic* standpoint the issues at stake are relatively straightforward. In a context where large numbers of Africans have historically moved, either temporarily or permanently, to seek opportunity or to expand their economic activity through trade, there has been almost continuous mixing of population, particularly in the cities. In some cases, certain occupations – traders, craftsmen, shopkeepers, drivers, gold dealers, and so forth – have 'traditionally' been in the hands of identifiable groups, either African or foreign (e.g. Lebanese, Indians). In others, people from a different territory have come as migrant workers (typically from poorer inland areas, such as Burkina Faso or Mali, to richer areas like Côte d'Ivoire or Senegal). Perhaps the most famous example of a successful economic enterprise of this type was that of the Gold Coast cocoa farmers, which required labour from outside the country. And the same applied to cocoa farming in the Côte d'Ivoire. Finally, there have always been itinerant traders or entrepreneurs, moving from area to area as seemed most opportune. Today the movement is faster and more extensive but the patterns of migration remain the same.

Such economic strangers have often settled down far from their community of origin and assimilated into the local groupings. The degree of assimilation and the form it took depended on local factors but it is fair to say that all African societies had mechanisms to integrate such outsiders. These ranged from the allocation of land for farming to the designation of particular social requirements for the practice of certain crafts, by way of the incorporation of slaves or labourers into local kinship networks. Over time some of those strangers assimilated fully and their descendants lost their links to their original locality. In other cases the distance between native and stranger remained, with continuous movement between place of origin and place of work, which kept alive a sense of foreignness. The difficulty is that perceptions of assimilation or foreignness were often different between the locals and the strangers and, more importantly, the criteria for identifying those differences changed over time.

Two economic issues appear to have sharpened the awareness of difference. The first has to do with the question of land; the second with what might be called occupational ascendancy. Where land has become scarce, and thereby more valuable, either in growing urban areas or in heavily cultivated regions, the question of ownership has become sharper. Given the lack of clear title deeds and the eminently contestable basis upon which land is allocated by chiefs, there is ample scope for dispute. And disputes of that type are more easily resolved by casting out those who can be identified as strangers. Similarly, in cases where some groups establish dominance in a particular economic activity – trade, shopkeeping or craftsmanship – increasing economic hardship leads readily to an attempt to reduce competition by removing those outside rivals. What is interesting here is that the criteria for identifying foreignness are instrumental: it is those who engage in certain economic activities who are deemed to be strangers, regardless of how thoroughly they may otherwise be assimilated. The recent expulsion of economic migrants in West Africa has been indiscriminate in this respect.

The *political* issue that has become increasingly common has turned on the use of national identity to remove political rivals from the scene. Whereas successful single-party politics put a premium on the cooptation of political rivals, multiparty elections engender rivalry. The (re-)emergence of competitive electoral systems in Africa has brought about a cut-throat competition between putative political rulers. In what has become an intense zero-sum game, all means (fair and foul) are used in order to prevail over political challengers.

Chief among those has been the use of foreignness. In almost all African countries, rules about citizenship and nationality have been revised and effectively narrowed so as to prevent some politicians from standing for office. These have ranged from a definition of nationality that required all four grandparents to be of that country – even if such a country did not exist before independence – to a requirement that one be born in the country in which one stands for election. The example of Côte d'Ivoire is probably the most notorious in this respect but there have been similar occurrences in Zambia and elsewhere.

Whatever the particulars of the case, these legal and constitutional twists have conspired to magnify the issue of origin and to sharpen (when not invent) a clear division between native and stranger. Beyond the fight for rulership, this political scramble for authenticity has affected numerous areas where party support divides along identity lines. The problem is twofold. First, there is disagreement about who is the original native in the region. Criteria based on chronological history clash with those of control and labour – that is, groups that may have come later but that have invested and transformed the area.[3] Second, the dominant local group expects its party to prevail in the game of representation. It does not take kindly to electoral defeat when that is the result of the fact that the so-called strangers, who do not identify with the local 'ethnic' party, have become more numerous – a reality that had not sunk in so dramatically until multiparty elections had taken place.

This is of course a problem that affects most cities in Africa since urbanisation on the continent has been massive and migrants come from all areas, in and out of the country. Potentially, therefore, every city in Africa where the (often self-appointed) natives have become a minority is a candidate for the politics of exclusion. Furthermore, there is now 'nativist' agitation even in areas where the distinction between indigenous and stranger had hitherto been muted, if not

3. This distinction is drawn from Lonsdale, 2008, which has been of great help for this whole section.

irrelevant. In this respect, it is clear that competitive multiparty politics have led to the rekindling of old disputes or the creation of identity conflicts that had not occurred before. The case of the 2008 elections in Kenya is emblematic of this problem, which now threatens stability in a number of African countries.

Finally, in a situation where economic circumstances are worsening, there has developed a new type of politics of violence based on a twisted form of identity politics. In cases, epitomised by Liberia and Sierra Leone, where the business of war becomes the new politics, the channels of violence are frequently gouged out of a simplistic definition of who is in and who is out. Here, the manufacture and abuse of rigid forms of identities, casting all strangers into legitimate targets, become political ends. Warlords resort to the crudest form of typecasting in order to justify acts of terror, the ultimate purpose of which is to gain control over marketable resources. However, in so doing they call upon notions of belonging that are distorted because they essentialise and instrumentalise attributes taken out of historical and cultural context. At its most extreme, the stranger is merely the individual who stands in the way.

These economic and political uses of the notion of stranger point back to its supposed *cultural* basis and bring once more to the fore the questions of origin, identity and belonging. Indeed, whatever the proximate reason for the stigmatisation of the stranger, the justification is always couched in terms that refer to cultural 'differences'. Of these, the most important has to do with belonging. By definition, the stranger does not belong, however well integrated (s)he may appear to be. Since the criteria for appurtenance may be convoluted, or even unclear, the task of identifying strangers will of necessity hark back to attributes that may in part be arbitrary – hence the difficulty for outsiders to make sense of the reasons given for exclusion. Although some of these are objectively defined, like nationality, others remain in the realm of self-fulfilling prophecy: they create the means by which to exclude previously identified 'others' one wished to reject anyway.

Of the more significant markers of 'foreignness', the two that are most immutable have to do with the land of the ancestors and the burial ground. These are indeed the ultimate tests of belonging. Those who have come from elsewhere have left their ancestors behind. There is nothing they can do about this; that tie can never be ignored or wilfully neglected. Migrants do return home to propitiate their ancestors and fulfil their obligations. Where the chain is broken, if it is broken, is with burial. If the natives have the edge in that they can identify their land with reference to their ancestors, they may well accept as native those strangers who are prepared to be buried in their place of adoption – for reasons of newly minted kinship or simply as a token of the permanence of their commitment to their present abode.

Yet, this is not as simple a matter as I am suggesting here, for the individual is not endowed with free will in this respect, on the model of what Western political theory intimates. In a very real sense, that choice is not the preserve of the single person; it has to arise out of the complex processes interlinking different registers of identity and origin that have intermingled sufficiently to allow for an individual to belong to a new and distinct place of 'origin'. This may occur through an inflected identification with the spouse's kin network, if that spouse is native; it may happen via occupational markers of identity that have local legitimacy; it might even be the result of particular forms of integration into local socio-political activities that imbue the stranger with a native dimension. In any event, this is an ancient process, which has made possible the vast intra-Africa migrations that are the hallmark of the continent. Myths of origin have always been sufficiently flexible to make possible 'rebirth' in a new location.

I have tried in this chapter to explain why belonging is both the most central of all human attributes and a flexible notion that allows a great deal of leeway in the ways it shapes identity. The saliency of current xenophobic activities is not to be explained merely in terms of the existence of 'differences', differences that have always been present in African societies, but by prevailing economic and political circumstances. They point to, but in no way exhaust, the nature of inter-group relations in a context where the failure to develop has conspired to increase poverty and reduce opportunities, thereby greatly aggravating competition for power and resources. In this context, the introduction of multiparty elections has engendered a dangerous dynamics of identity violence because it has encouraged politicians to campaign on nativist issues and to seek local votes by decrying strangers. This has created new tensions and revived (or invented) historical grievances, which could undo much of the achievements of post-colonial national integration.

THREE

The politics of believing

Following what has been in the previous two chapters a necessary but somewhat artificial division between the various attributes of the person and the relations between individuals and groups, this chapter aims to bring all these separate elements together. Both what a person is and how he or she belongs to the various groupings that come to make him/her an individual are conditioned by the belief system within which people make sense of and conduct their lives. This is true everywhere, of course, but I am here concerned to understand how the specificities of what might be called the politics of contemporary African lives hinge on the question of belief. By belief I refer to the whole of the spiritual world: this clearly concerns religion but is not confined to it; it also includes what is sometimes called the universe of the spirits or the occult. Therefore, it requires a way of looking at religion as being composed of different facets, many of which may have little to do with churches or institutionalised doctrine.

This is an area on which political theories of Africa have fairly circumscribed views. In most instances belief is equated with either religion or values. In the first case, political scientists are interested in the influence of religious creeds and of churches on politics. In the second, they consider belief to be synonymous with value – that is, a particular set of foundational positions that incite people to behave in certain ways. Clearly, there is nothing wrong in studying churches or values but these are categories of analysis that leave out too much of what matters in Africa's spiritual world. Any attempt to understand this world ought to start from a consideration of what makes sense to people on the ground. This means keeping an open mind about that which constitutes a belief and making the effort of interpreting the political relevance of beliefs without resorting to the crippling analytical dichotomy of 'tradition' versus 'modernity.'

One of the hurdles here has to do with the division of labour between Africanist disciplines. It is customary for political science to dwell on the overtly political aspects of social life and to leave the study of the spiritual world to either anthropology or theology. This has led to a situation where it is assumed by political scientists that questions of religious beliefs and spirituality have but marginal relevance and that whatever relevance they have belongs to the realm of the private sphere or the esoteric. However, this is of more than disciplinary concern since it engenders assumptions both about what is rational or irrational and about the political significance of religion. Whereas political scientists readily accept that economic issues are directly relevant to politics, they are much more resistant to the notion that the world of beliefs is of equal importance. To put it in crude terms: political *science* does not do 'voodoo'. Unfortunately for political scientists, 'voodoo' does politics.

For this reason, I want here to give attention to three important aspects of religion that are rarely discussed by Africanist political scientists: *morality, rationality* and *agency*. These would normally be the preserve of different disciplines: theology, economics, philosophy and psychology. My choice of themes is not coincidental; it reflects an effort on my part to bring into political analysis aspects that are often left out but that clearly have lasting importance for politics. As ever, my concern is not to provide cast-iron definitions of these three concepts but to reflect on what they may mean in contemporary Africa. I am not primarily concerned here with hermeneutics but, more modestly, with trying to uncover what these three spheres of existence represent to ordinary people in their everyday life. Nor am I writing of 'African' morality, rationality or action. I am offering an analysis of morality, rationality and action in the African post-colonial context.

MORALITY

Although the question of morality is hardly broached explicitly in Africanist political science, it is in fact the elephant in the room. To take but two examples: not only is there constant reference to violence on the continent, much of which is seen by outsiders as peculiarly vicious or 'barbaric', but there is an equal obsession about politicians' lack of moral integrity, which is frequently seen to be at the root of the corruption that undermines development. Often such unpalatable behaviour is laid at the door of backward traditions, which are believed to compel and constrain political behaviour in negative ways. Such explanations are culturalist by default since they do not openly acknowledge the role of culture but nevertheless refer to it as an explanation, albeit of last resort. Politics in Africa lack morality, it is suggested, because African beliefs are obsolete – which is another way of saying that 'traditional' beliefs are not suited to the morality of the 'modern' world.

If we are to move from such a narrow and ethnocentric vision of Africa, we need to revisit the question of morality in its complex contemporary forms. To do so it is useful to examine more carefully the relationship between three of its central components: *religion, tradition* and *obligation*. I want to try to understand here the ways in which morality derives from the working out of religious beliefs within the parameters of tradition and obligation that define individuals. The point of approaching morality in this way is to stress its multi-stranded nature and its complex composition, making for a mix of norms and beliefs which may not always be easily compatible. The disjuncture of these three aspects, which is the hallmark of (particularly post-colonial) societies in rapid transition, is one reason why there appear to be competing moralities or at least competing systems of 'traditional' and 'modern' beliefs intersecting and, to some extent, interfering with each other.

It is not just the fact that Africa is home to a vast number of religions – ranging from the established Christian and Islamic churches to a large number of native Christian sects and Pentecostal movements – which singles out the continent. Rather, it is that different types of religion intermingle – by which I mean that the established world religions and the more recent native churches have built upon, rather than displaced, what are called 'traditional' religious beliefs. If sometimes this has produced syncretic variants of established churches, more often than not it has resulted in a form of religion that has married official rituals with unofficial practices. Even Islam and some of the more unbending Protestant churches have had to propitiate native religious obligations – for instance towards ancestors – and indulge indigenous 'traditions' such as female genital mutilation. These practices may well be attributed to customs rather than beliefs but it is doubtful whether the two can so easily be dissociated. Customs are always underpinned by a system of morality that explains and justifies. When the universal churches dogmatically dismiss such customs, they lose purchase and are diminished as the moral framework for living. In Africa, imported religions adapt or shrivel.

Modernisers, both in Africa and outside, are impatient with customs they see as so many impediments to the adoption of a more modern and universal morality, one that is compatible with the socio-economic and political changes required for development. They fail to understand that religion is the glue that binds communities together and that it can only evolve in consonance – not against – societal transformation. Morality is thus no more 'traditional' than the society of which it is a part. The choice is not between a more or less 'modern' morality but between a society with or without morality. The events that have taken place in countries where the glue of 'traditional' morality has dissolved (e.g. Mozambique, Sudan, Liberia, Zaire/DRC, Sierra Leone) show clearly what consequences the contempt of tradition may bring forth.

It is thus important to pay greater attention to the positive and constructive side of 'traditional' morality, rooted as it is in local religion and customary systems of reciprocal obligation. In point of fact, a more nuanced analysis of post-colonial Africa would reveal that political morality is more often the result of the application of 'traditional' norms and beliefs than that of the more 'modern' ones that are supposed to sustain today's liberal democratic politics. It has been suggested that whatever political accountability obtained in contemporary Africa was rooted in the ethnic moral and political economy.[1] Equally, some have shown that there were informal or 'traditional' forms of accountability that had greater purchase than the formally institutionalised ones.[2] In both instances, accountability is more effective for being part of the morality of a tradition of reciprocal obligation that continues to have a compelling presence.

In a different register, two forms of 'traditional' justice have contributed greatly to the refashioning of societal morality after an orgy of cataclysmic violence had threatened to obliterate it. In Mozambique, rituals of forgiveness and purification have made possible the reintegration of child killers, who had otherwise lost all claims to the humanity that is central to the notion of being.[3] Such ceremonies have achieved far more than all the worthwhile, and no doubt useful, psychological counselling provided by foreign NGOs to former child soldiers. In Rwanda, the *gacaca* tribunals, which are rooted in 'traditional' systems of local justice, are not just the only realistic way of bringing to justice the thousands who are charged with having committed atrocities but they are also the only reliable path towards some (albeit limited) form of reconciliation.[4] Here,

---

1. Lonsdale, 1995, 2003.
2. Kelsall, 2004.
3. Honwana, 2005.
4. Gabisirege and Babalola, 2001.

then, are concrete examples of morality in action that use 'traditional' notions of identity, behaviour and belonging to contribute to the resolution of 'modern' ethical and social issues.

Beyond these exceptional cases, however, it is also essential to approach morality as the framework within which people in general, and politicians in particular, make decisions. One example above all illustrates the complexities of the issue. Clientelism is considered nefarious to good governance and so it may be in the narrow political science notion of what a properly accountable democratic political system ought to be. But let us consider for an instant what the morality of clientelism entails within the political dispensation of contemporary African countries. Understanding how clientelism is experienced by African men and women today means looking simultaneously at the ethics of modern politics and the morality of virtuous behaviour within a world of reciprocity.

The ethics of modern politics, in Africa as elsewhere, lie in the compact between citizens and government. More or less freely chosen leaders commit themselves more or less to manage national resources wisely and to look after the well-being of the citizens. They operate within relatively well-defined administrative and judicial constraints, which make them accountable to the population. Elections adjudicate between competing politicians and competing programmes. However, this 'morality' is undermined by a number of critical factors, of which the culture of reciprocity is not the least important. What happens is that the compact of modern politics is not necessarily seen, either by the politicians or by the citizens, as the bedrock of the common good. It is but one of many mechanisms of representation that need to be adapted to the demands of a more fundamental morality in which rulers and ruled are linked within a world of obligation that is at the core of what is called clientelism. So, right from the start there is a collision between two different types of political ethics, which in real life are completely intertwined.

Therefore, the reasoning that consists in associating 'modern' political morality with progress (i.e. development) and 'traditional'

ethics with backwardness is flawed. First, it fails to consider that
what makes the 'modern' liberal-democratic dispensation desirable
is less its morality than its management efficiency in the running
of institutionalised organisations based on bureaucratic rather than
personal logic. Hence, it is not that elections are 'morally' superior;
it is the fact that elections are part of a political system in which
accountability is conceptualised in terms, and enforceable by means,
of elections. However, in a situation where competing notions of
accountability offer much richer and seemingly more appropriate
alternatives to elections as a means of selecting and influencing
representatives, morality is not necessarily best served by multiparty
electoral means.

Second, it assumes that 'traditional' political morality is incompatible with 'modern' governance – which is only true in tautological
terms, since what passes for modern is but the evolution of Western,
rather than African, traditions of government. Moreover, it is plainly
wrong in circumstances where the so-called 'modern' political institutions have acquired only limited legitimacy, in part because
their morality is not obvious to the bulk of the population. Indeed,
when politicians obey the commands of 'traditional' reciprocity
more firmly than they discharge their 'modern' democratic duties,
it is only natural that clientelism should appear to be both more
moral and more practical. Since the crisis of governance in Africa is
undoubtedly due to the failings of 'modern' political accountability
– which is either weak or non-existent – it is natural that people
want the 'traditional' morality of the accountability of clientelism
to continue to prevail. In this case, as in many others, morality and
rationality go hand in hand.

RATIONALITY

In political science, the notion of rationality is most forcefully
associated with rational choice theories, which have narrowed the
definition of the term to that of the maximisation of individual

preferences. Whether rational choice theories apply to a wide range of political settings and not just to Western liberal democracies is a question I will not debate here.[5] But such theories nevertheless rest on key assumptions, which do require discussion. For our purposes, the foundational axioms of rational choice have to do with particular notions of the individual, of maximisation and of self-interest that are highly contestable in many non-Western settings. To take but one example: if the meaning of self-interest has to be inserted into the reality of the 'communal' individual and the morality of reciprocity, then it is difficult to conceive of a straightforward application of the concept of rationality advocated by such theories.

This would not matter so much if it were only a question of theory. However, such assumptions about rationality are at the core of most Africanist political theories even when they remain wholly implicit. For this reason, it is important to offer an alternative view of rationality that is in greater consonance with the present circumstances on the continent. This suggests a conceptualisation of the notion that fits with the contemporary politics of belonging. In this view, rationality is the application of logical reasoning to a political realm that rests on the virtue of the collective social good and the morality of the reciprocity that binds rulers and ruled in a highly hybrid form of political accountability. What is rational in such a context is likely to appear 'irrational' to Western political theory, as I show by looking in greater detail at two aspects of rationality that find no place in such theory: *gift* and *witchcraft*. I have chosen these two examples *not* because they are necessarily representative of present-day politics in Africa but because they illustrate the challenge faced by Africanist political theories when trying to account for what happens on the continent.

As anthropologists have detailed, the prevalence of *gift* or *giving* in 'traditional' societies is to be explained in terms of a political economy of exchange and reciprocity that is alien to commodity trade and profit-making. It is part of an array of obligations that

---

5. This is discussed in depth in Chabal and Daloz, 2006.

sustain identity, virtue and good relations within a group and between communities. However, most social scientific interpretations
of gift centre on the instrumentally rational nature of what serves
both as social lubricant and as an incipient form of social security.
Further, they assume that the practice of giving becomes less relevant
as other more 'modern' forms of socio-political exchange and protection emerge. But this will not do.

I would like to highlight another aspect that is equally important
but fails to figure in present accounts of African post-colonial politics:
that is, the intimate connection between giving, being and belonging. My point is that giving is not merely instrumental but also
constitutive of the very identity of the individual-within-the-group.
The purpose of the gift is not just to act as a social hedge against
future fortune; it is also a core component of self-identification and
of the assessment of the morality of the 'others'. If such is the case,
then, the assumption that the rationale of gift exchange will wither
with the consolidation of the 'modern' commodity-based capitalist
political economy does not hold so neatly.

The fact that giving is an integral part of the politics of being
and belonging makes its continuation contingent on much slower,
and more subterranean, changes in the ways in which people define
themselves and measure others. Far from being 'mechanically' related to the development of a capitalist economy, the evolution of
the political economy of giving is in fact linked to the vagaries of
the process of individualisation taking place in Africa. Changes in
respect of the formation and evolution of the person, which depend
on myriad non-economic factors, are likely to occur at an entirely
different pace from those of market forces or trade patterns.

To show that the existing notion of individual is to a greater or
lesser extent communal is obviously not to suggest either that this
constitutes the 'essence' of the individual in Africa or, even less,
that it is a timeless such attribute. The argument here is not that the
notion of the social person is not evolving in Africa, and in many
ways evolving in the direction of types of individualisation that have

occurred elsewhere. It is to make clear that the assumptions made in respect either of the concept of the individual or about the rationality of the political are simply not warranted in current circumstances.

It is not acceptable for Africanist political scientists to presume that the concept of individual they use is unproblematic. What matters about the process of individualisation in Africa is not so much how it may conform to patterns found elsewhere but how it differs, for it is in the differences that lies the material from which it becomes possible to fashion an interpretation of politics that does actually account for what takes place locally. Similarly, it is vital to place the analysis of rationality within the study of the whole realm of beliefs, which codify social behaviour and political expectations.

In this context, then, the politics of giving – that is, of material reciprocity – are of the utmost importance. Integrating an exploration of the role of gift within the prevailing 'traditional' political economy enables us to tease out the complexities of current political rationalities. This allows for a finer-grain appreciation of the shades of grey to be found among local politicians, some of whom might be acting 'honourably', even if outside the bounds of constitutional propriety, whereas others may be abusing the legitimacy of the rationality of reciprocity.

For example, it it is clear that the erstwhile ruler of Côte d'Ivoire, Houphouët-Boigny, commonly assessed as a consummate opportunist and petty tyrant, was in fact a far more complex character. He was, until the last ten years of his life, a master politician who managed to combine like few others control over a relatively efficient 'modern' state and the workings of a more 'traditional' political economy of reciprocity. He was able to integrate the attributes of the wise, benevolent, 'traditional' chief with the qualities of the experienced 'modern' politician who had mastered the intricacies of parliamentary and electoral politics as an MP in the French parliament and a minister in the French government. Events in Côte d'Ivoire since his death have made plain how skilful he had been in his ruthless determination to play the hybrid politics that suited the setting in which he was operating. His patent failure in the twilight of his reign should not detract from his real achievements, and his real popularity, during the twenty years that followed independence.[6]

Perhaps even more controversially, I would suggest that political theories of Africa need to provide plausible accounts of the political rationality of *witchcraft*.[7] The fact that this is a topic on which Africanist political science is virtually silent is in itself significant, for it illustrates most graphically the sheer limitations of political theories that either dismiss such questions as irrelevant or are simply incapable of providing an analysis of their relevance by means of existing methodologies. Yet, to confine witchcraft entirely to the realm of the 'irrational' is to neglect a whole area of cultural and socio-political action that rests on well-understood relations of dependence and reciprocity within actually existing, as opposed to long disappeared, societies.

Here too there is a substantial anthropological corpus, much of which developed within a vision of 'traditional' society that was both essentialist and static, but which still has some relevance for current analysis.[8] However, it is the recent work on the 'modernity' of witchcraft that provides the most interesting material for political theory.[9] Far from disappearing from the social scene, as had universally been predicted by theories of modernisation, witchcraft in Africa has 'mutated' in a way that has made it entirely germane to 'modern' politics. Indeed, the practices of witchcraft have adapted to the capitalist economy, electoral politics and even the spread of new technologies in communication. It is able to provide believable accounts of events and processes within the three 'modern' spheres of modern life – economy, politics and communication – that offer both explanation and remedy.

---

6. Of course, to explain his success is not to condone his politics; it is to provide a more plausible account than those which have seen in him merely a devious dictator.

7. However controversial the use of that concept, I shall use it here and in the remainder of the book simply because there is no other that is more satisfactory.

8. Evans-Pritchard, 1937.

9. Geschiere, 1997.

I have detailed elsewhere how witchcraft can serve at least three purposes in contemporary African life: healing, accountability and social leveller.[10] The first facilitates what in the West would be called the psychological resolution of everyday problems – that is, provide therapy for illness, trauma, death or simply bad luck. Witchcraft can offer treatment for psychological or social disorder – especially in urban settings where such problems are more widespread and more acute. The second can be used to force politicians to fulfil their obligations of reciprocity at the local level, no matter how elevated their station and arbitrary their rule. Since their legitimacy as representatives is firmly tied to their local roots, any attempt to neglect their community of origin can be sanctioned by accusations of witchcraft, which they must take seriously. This can act as a form of accountability, albeit of a kind invisible to the Africanist political scientist. The third is a means of exercising pressure on those who are wealthy so that they redistribute some of their riches to their locality of origin – in keeping with the features of the politics of belonging discussed above. Here too, it might be argued that it serves that aspect of political representation which stresses the politician's obligations to his/her local kinship group.

This is by no means an exhaustive account of the socio-political role of witchcraft in contemporary Africa, merely some telling examples. My point here is simply, but firmly, to explain that the study of the rationality of witchcraft (and other forms of belief that are habitually billed as 'occult') is not only judicious but that it ought to be an integral part of any serious political theory of the continent. Because the salience and modalities of witchcraft differ vastly in different settings, they need to be analysed in their local context. What is not in dispute, however, is that it belongs to a sphere of rationality that is rarely taken into account by Africanist political theories. Witchcraft is definitely not irrational.

---

10. Chabal and Daloz, 1999: ch. 5.

AGENCY

I now want to return to the question of agency, which I discussed in some detail in the Introduction. What I want to understand here is how matters of belief, as they work themselves through the context of the politics of being and belonging, affect politics. I am thinking here primarily of how the spiritual world in which people live and work shapes the way they understand, and participate in, politics. Taken in this broader sense, the question becomes that of considering the limits of political *action* within a spiritual realm that conditions issues of ethics. Although I am not seeking here to ferret out the equivalent in Africa of the 'Protestant ethic', which Weber saw as a key factor in the rise of capitalism, I do want to understand how best to approach the broad issue of agency.

Again, Africanist political science is not very helpful here since it works on the assumption that human beings everywhere are similarly motivated to act, or labour, even if it is recognised that culture and history have a role to play. Perhaps a good example of the limits of such political theories in respect of Africa is class analysis, which held sway from the 1960s to the 1980s – and still has purchase today. Class analysis is as unambiguous a theory of action as there is, since it asserts the economic causalities that induce particular social and political behaviour. The debate here is not so much about class analysis per se but about the relevance of its application to post-colonial Africa. Here, it might be argued not just that class analysis was making assumptions that were not justified but also that its focus on the parameters of class formation distracted political analysis from what was actually taking place.

I have discussed class analysis in detail elsewhere.[11] Here, I merely want to explain why it was deficient. This was not so much because classes had not yet consolidated in Africa but rather that even where they had begun to materialise Africans continued largely to behave according to 'traditional' social, cultural and economic logics that

---

11. Chabal, 1994: 15–19.

class analysis supposed were being transcended. In this sense, it appeared that labouring within a capitalist economy did not produce classes, at least not classes that behaved like classes! Leaving aside whether capitalism had actually permeated post-colonial Africa or even whether class analysis is an accurate account of what happened in the Ur-capitalist countries of Western Europe, my point here is merely to expose the limits of Western political theories as they were applied to Africa. What is true of class analysis is also true of development theory, dependency theory and democratic theory. All share a view of the causality of social, economic and political action which is singularly dismissive of actual historical and cultural processes on the ground. Africans are fitted into a pre-existing mould; their agency is predetermined.

My intention, then, is to approach the question of social, economic and political action from a local perspective. And I want to begin with matters of belief, religion and ethics. My aim is not to unearth the factors that cause action as such; it is merely to set the ethical stage upon which agency is played out. Of particular importance in this respect are three issues: the understanding of the *cycle of life*, the notion of *public virtue*, and the concept of the *public good*. What, in other words, are the connections between ethics and agency? For me, therefore, ethics are not easily dissociated from culture, and culture is but a vast network of symbols or, as Geertz put it in a formulation that has its origins in Weber, a vast web of meanings.[12]

By *cycle of life*, I mean to reflect the compelling force of man's conceptualisation of his place in the universe upon his behaviour. It has often been said, and may be no less true for having become a cliché, that a belief in reincarnation has made possible the maintenance of a caste system in India that has long induced a degree of fatalism. This does not imply that India will forever remain prisoner of this religious curse, as clearly it is not; it means only that an understanding of India's evolution in the last hundred years needs to

---

12. Geertz, 1973: 'Thick Description: Toward an Interpretive Theory of Culture', p. 5.

take seriously the weight of such beliefs. In Africa, religion rests on a vision of the cycle of life that gives primacy to the idea that living and dead inhabit the same world, or, to put it another way, that the dead continue to play an active part in the affairs of the community. Of course, such beliefs are by no means specific to Africa – that is not my point – but in so far as they matter to Africans, then we must try to assess their importance.

This vision of the cycle of life stresses an ethics, which puts a premium on the upholding of a certain number of foundational principles having to do with respect for age, the elders and, more generally, matters of long tradition. Although this is a generalisation that may not apply equally well to all areas of Africa, it is certainly of relevance in large parts of it. Only local research can confirm or invalidate it. However, there is certainly evidence that it does impinge on local frameworks of action, for instance through such phenomena as the belief in the power of spirits, the deference afforded elder statesmen, the continued significance of 'traditional' status or rank, the need to favour place of origin, the reluctance to accept strangers as genuine political representatives, the adaptation of universal religions to local precepts, the requirement for politicians to submit to local rituals and accept local spiritual authority, as well as the ubiquitous resort by national leaders to 'advisers' who are supposed to placate the forces of the occult.

I am aware that reference to such factors may appear facetious in what is supposed to be a study of political theory. I am also aware that such remarks might easily be hijacked by those who want to paint a picture of Africa as being backward. To these charges there are two answers. The first is that all parts of the world are, or have been, similarly affected by their religious and ethical beliefs. It is clear, for instance, that what appears to many as wholly irrational religious dogma (such as 'creationism') on the part of the religious fundamentalists in the United States has a direct bearing on crucial issues of society and politics – not to mention international relations. The second is that it is never possible to endow matters of beliefs and religion with (straightforward) causal force – as even Weber realised in his discussion of the Protestant ethic. To situate social and political action within a discussion of belief systems is not to imply that these factors are causally determinant; merely that they have a relevance that needs to be teased out in the finer-grain analysis of the local.

This African ethical framework of action also implies a 'conservative' notion of politics in so far as it is difficult to justify change that is not consonant with proper respect for this view of the cycle of life. It is simply not 'moral' needlessly to upset the order of the spiritual. This is not to say that the ancestors would object to nuclear power or electoral competition – as some simple-minded observers of Africa might infer – but only that the scope and reach of options open to social and political reformers in Africa are constrained in ways that link up to this ethics of life. I leave to others the judgement of whether this is favourable or not to the flowering of market capitalism and liberal democracy.

It is more important for our purpose to try to understand what an appreciation of local ethics means for public virtue in Africa, for virtue has always been a guide to social and political action. By public virtue I mean the qualities of those who exercise leadership in public life. Or, to put it another way, what turns power into authority? What makes social or political action worthy of praise? Neglected as this area is by standard Africanist political theories, it is quite critical to the assessment of the achievements of public figures in today's Africa. I have already shown how notions of representation and legitimacy were tied to the attributes of the person who is entrusted with political action. I want now to suggest that the definition of what constitutes a desirable course of action and of the criteria for the measurement of achievement must be congruent with ethical notions of public virtue.

The first element has to do with the practical consequences of the dominance of a political economy of reciprocity. It is more honourable to recirculate than to accumulate wealth. Or, rather, it is acceptable to accumulate wealth only if it is intended to redistribute it; otherwise it offends public virtue. This means that there is a premium on being generous, rather than efficient. Success is not measured by the accumulation of wealth but by its wise dispersion. A virtuous person is munificent. This state of affairs has two immediate effects. One is that there is no intrinsic virtue in accumulation for investment or in deferring expenditure – business people are routinely expected to sacrifice economic efficiency or long-term planning for instant largesse. Another is that status is not attached to wealth per se but to its visible use, particularly its appropriate distribution.

The second element is that the success of an individual action – whether social, political or economic – is measured not in individualist but in communal terms. Public virtue consists not in personal achievement per se but in what that achievement conveys and embodies for the locality of which the individual is a part. This means not just that material benefits must be shared but that the attributes of success only translate into public recognition, status or respect if they can be reinterpreted in communal language. 'Modern' public recognition must be sustained by 'traditional' public validation, which is only bestowed if and when the injunctions of the group's ethics have been followed. This means that those who succeed away from home, particularly abroad, are still expected to meet local normative standards if they are to have their achievements endorsed by the community and turned into a capital of public virtue, or social capital. Those who have been successful are not necessarily admired; they may be feared. If they want to become virtuous they must submit to the local ethics of their community. In this way, at least, social or political action, change and reform are filtered by the gatekeepers of 'tradition'.

This notion of virtue has direct bearing on the concept of the *public good* – by which I mean specifically what it is that is seen to be collectively desirable. To what main aims should socio-economic or political agency be directed? The pursuit of the public good is, in every society, the mark of political legitimacy. Can it be the case that some rulers are short of legitimacy at the local level but create for themselves an overall national authority by devoting themselves to what is consensually accepted as the public good? The question here, therefore, is to attempt to work out how that is defined and measured; how action is validated by communities and society alike in the ethical context I have presented. This raises the issue of the homogeneity of African countries: can the different groupings that form a country agree on what the public good is? To what extent are politicians able to combine the demands of local reciprocity with a larger commitment to the national 'interest'?

This is a complex matter since it might be argued that there can be no concept of 'public' good in an environment where local considerations always trump supra- or trans-local ones. Africanist political theory usually skirts around this problem, by positing a number of universal public goods such as health, lodging, work and basic human rights, which all societies must desire and towards which all politicians must strive. However, above and beyond the requirements of what might be called basic natural rights, such as to make survival and the prospect of a better life possible, there is a distinct lack of consensus on what the public good might actually be. Or, rather, it is difficult to determine what it is other than in the specific local context. To some extent, then, the question of the nature of the public good is best left to actual research in the field. It is better not to presume to know what groups of people will value most highly, and even less to assume – as is political scientists' wont – what the public aims of 'modern' politicians should be.

Yet, in a context where all African countries are also 'modern' environments, where people do aspire to a better life and to a share in the bounties of modernisation that are so visible to them worldwide, the issue of the public good cannot simply be limited to a relativist notion of what is prized locally. And, indeed, African politicians are constantly confronted with the tensions between the multiple, overlapping and not always compatible ideas of what the most pressing and desirable public goods ought to be. Whereas notions of public virtue are primarily informed by the ethics of local life, ideas of the public good are more diverse. Hence, it may be helpful to speak of the development of hybrid concepts, drawn from 'tradition' and 'modernity', formal and informal: what is thought should constitute the public good is the product of the reciprocal influence of local and global aspirations on the ethical sphere that guides action.

This creates a double standard. On the one hand, people expect action to conform to the accepted norms of public virtue. On the other, they want results. The outcome is that politicians often operate on a double basis. They try to address national issues of, say, development and poverty alleviation, so as to improve conditions in the country as a whole. At the same time, they privilege those policies that enhance their local standing, and thereby increase their own personal virtue. One direct consequence of this policy is that they almost always seek to gain personal credit for those initiatives that can demonstrably be seen to improve local conditions. The new hospital is not the outcome of the health ministry's plan; it is the personal gift of the local politician. The same goes for schools, roads, and all conceivable manner of economic improvement schemes.

This hybridised notion of the public good makes manifest and maintains a system of public policy that is ill suited to the type of national action plan for development which most African countries need. 'Development' translates in practice into the material advantage sought and obtained by the various groupings to which the politicians belong or to which they are beholden. This does not mean that there is no effort on the part of government to devise, and implement, policies that benefit the country as a whole. What it does mean is that the implementation of such policies is subjected not just to the greed of local demand but also, and more problematically, to competing notions of public good that politicians find almost impossible to resist. Therefore, the difficulty lies less in the inherent corruption of political leadership in Africa – however acute that might be – than in the systemic contradictions inherent in the translation of the local ethics of public virtue into a more coherent, national and long-term vision of the public good.

Although it may appear that this chapter has given undue emphasis to what are often seen by political scientists as 'traditional' beliefs, it has in fact sought to make plain why questions of belief, rationality and virtue matter. Only when we make the effort to understand the moral, religious and ethical dimensions of political action can we begin to account for behaviour that is all too often relegated to the realm of caricature. Whatever the nature of political failings in contemporary Africa, we must try to use analytical instruments that enable us to discriminate more accurately between what is legitimate and illegitimate political behaviour and to make sense of the extent to which political discourse is consonant with local beliefs and expectations. Only then will we be in a position to assess the limits of current politics on the continent.

FOUR

The politics of partaking

The previous three chapters, which went together, may well have given the impression of an Africa that is both 'traditional' and static – seeing that they sought to discuss the politics of being, belonging and believing in analytically clear, but ostensibly synchronic, terms. It is time to pause, therefore, and recast our enterprise in light of what these chapters have brought to the analysis of politics in post-colonial Africa. It is also time to address directly the question of stasis, or timelessness, which has long plagued Africanist writing. Finally, it is time to bring culture into political analysis. The present chapter starts from where the previous one left off – agency and political action – but before developing my argument further I would like to raise the issue of how best to interpret the dynamics of an Africa that appears to be caught in its 'traditions'.

The dilemma for the analyst is either to pretend such 'traditions' do not exist or to explain them away in terms of a theory of progress that relegates them to a past eventually to be overcome by modernisation. This will not do and we need to confront the issue of 'tradition' squarely. I want to argue that it is possible *both* to make the effort of accounting for traditions *and* to avoid turning them into a causality of backwardness, doom and despair. What this requires is an approach to the question by way of culture – defined as both substantive and dynamic. I draw here on three conclusions reached in an earlier book.[1]

The first is that an approach to culture based on the interpretation of meanings gives ample leeway for an account of change – since theory is informed by the observation of what is happening on the ground. The second is that making explicit the cultural framework within which meaning is imparted is not to reify that framework but to try to account for the way it changes over time. The last is that such a cultural approach puts a premium on avoiding ossifying dichotomies such as 'tradition' and 'modernity' since it calls for an explanation of change that looks at how specific 'modernities' are rooted in their own 'traditions'.

What the first three chapters did, then, was to set the scene upon which action unfolds – that is, they sought to highlight the webs of meaning within which individuals and groups act in the world. That the scene is as it is obviously has direct relevance to what *may* take place there but it does not determine what *will* take place. The charge that the attempt to explain how people make sense of, and behave within, their world is to make them the puppets of existing 'traditions' is patently absurd since all of us operate within our own context of meanings, or culture. Of course, all of us can become uncomfortable when analysis brings to light the cultural matrix within which we live – uncomfortable for the simple reason that analysis points to areas of our lives of which we may not be aware or about which we are sensitive. But we cannot reject such readings only because they are offered by outsiders. The only relevant critique of an approach in terms of the interpretation of meanings is whether it is an accurate, or at least plausible, account of what is at stake. And the only way to make progress in this debate is to confront differing accounts of particular processes.

My argument is that what the three previous chapters offer by way of the interpretation of meanings is both apposite and heuristically

---

1. Chabal and Daloz, 2006.

relevant to the explanation of political action. In this chapter I cast the analytical beacon upon some of the ways in which individuals in contemporary Africa *partake* in politics. What I mean by 'partake' is *both* and *simultaneously* 'take part in' and 'make use of' – a deliberately ambiguous notion intended to convey the complex relationships between individuals-within-groups and the world of politics, or rather the world of politicians. Again, I have privileged an outlook from the ground up rather than the more familiar political science top-down approach. Therefore, I am less interested in how the state seeks to capture and incorporate politically the country's population than in how people relate to the vagaries of contemporary politics as they wash over them. To this end, I do not look at individuals only as 'modern' political actors – discrete members of a polity in which they play the part allotted to them by political theory – but try instead to understand how they make sense of, and cope with, the political game as it has evolved since independence.

The starting point is an analysis of how individuals, as defined in the first three chapters, have been involved in politics since the colonial period. This historical approach is one way of trying to assess what I believe to be three of the most significant types of relationship between the powerful and the powerless, the rulers and the ruled, the politicians and the populace: that is, as *subject*, *client* and *citizen*. Of course, this does not exhaust the relations between top and bottom, elites and ordinary people, rich and poor, and so on. It is merely a way of focusing attention on those types of entanglements that are distinctly political – even if in each case there is more to simple politics, or, to put it another way, that politics itself overlaps with other spheres of life.

SUBJECT

The notion of subject is not commonly used in contemporary comparative political science, since it is generally assumed that this refers to an age when rulers were kings who had political dominion over their populace. That relationship, most often seen as marking the feudal age, defined subjects as those whose rights were limited to the protection of the suzerain in exchange for a bundle of economic, social and political obligations. It is the tacit assumption of current political theory that individuals no longer stand in such relation vis-à-vis their rulers, who are now chosen by means of elections and whose legitimacy lies in that democratic compact. Leaving aside the discussion of whether, other than in Ethiopia, there was anything resembling a feudal order in pre-colonial Africa, it is worth revisiting the question of subject within the pre-colonial and colonial context.

If in pre-colonial Africa there were well-established kingdoms, of which the Muslim emirates were perhaps the most modern, there were numerous features that differed significantly from Europe. Of those, the following are relevant to a consideration of what a subject has been in Muslim Africa since the nineteenth century. Africans had greater leeway in moving between kingdoms and the other, less centralised, polities. Their allegiance to Islam was always more syncretic and less constraining – religion was not the rigid and frightening world-view it was in Europe. Their obligations were usually more fluid and flexible since rulers sought wealth primarily for status and less frequently for warfare. Finally, they largely continued to live and work according to the moral and ethical framework that pre-dated the advent of Islam. In short, subjecthood was far less totalising than in Europe or, for that matter, the Islamic Middle East.

Other than in the Islamic states, and Ethiopia, people in Africa were thus not subjects in the sense it is usually understood in European history. However, they certainly became subjects of the empire when they came under colonial rule – and this in more than rhetorical fashion. The colonial state acted like a feudal lord in many significant respects. Here, being a subject meant becoming tributary to a centralised state that sought to exercise absolute, unaccountable and largely arbitrary power over virtually every aspect of people's lives. The fact that the colonial authorities were primarily interested

in extracting maximum resources from the least financial and coercive expenditure meant that they usually exercised a relatively
benign type of authoritarian rule. Nevertheless, when called upon
the state could be as callous and brutal as feudal lords had been
in earlier times: violence was both endemic and systematic in the
colonial world.

What matters for our purposes is not so much the exact nature of
colonial rule as the understanding of how the identity of the colonial
subject impinged upon and reshaped the relation between people
and the centre of power. Being a colonial subject was a confusing
and contradictory business. Colonial governments wanted both that
Africans should continue to conduct their lives according to the
'traditions' that kept a social order easier to control and that they
should obey the more categorical strictures of 'modern' citizenship.
This dichotomy was institutionalised by means of the distinction
made, in legal terms, between 'native' and 'civilised' – as the French
and Portuguese were wont to classify the Africans. The British had
more subtle ways of signifying emancipation from 'tradition' but the
upshot was the same.

This resulted in what one scholar has defined as a split between
'citizen' and 'subject'.[2] The former were integrated into the modern
body politic; the latter were left to the vagaries of customary law,
enforced with some considerable leeway by (real or appointed)
chiefs. This is true as far as it goes but such a distinction should
not be overplayed. Whatever the details, the consequence of colonial
rule was in this respect to place those Africans who were not part
of the emerging political elite in a position of double subjection:
'modern' and 'traditional'. Modern in that the colonial state evolved a
form of governance that paid little heed to accountability. Africans
thus found themselves the subjects of this 'modern' state with little
to say about either its workings or its policies. Traditional in that the
colonial system also largely removed the accountability mechanisms

---

2. Mamdani, 1996.

that had linked chiefs and subjects in pre-colonial Africa. Colonial or colonially approved chiefs were in effect auxiliaries of the colonial state, to which they were accountable, in the person of the district officer.

Far from bestowing on Africans political emancipation, colonial rulers thus instituted a dual form of subjecthood, which undermined their modernising discourse and created a bastard form of political control. The efforts on the eve of decolonisation to turn this hybrid system, hitherto entirely geared to the ease of colonial administration, into a more accountable and more manageable type of government moulded on the metropolitan achieved only superficial success. Promised the political kingdom upon the withdrawal of the colonial overlord, Africans quickly found out that they remained the subjects of the now independent state. The hybrid system that had combined the 'modern' and 'traditional' to keep them in their place during the colonial period was now adjusted to the realities of post-colonial rule. The blend was distinct but the outcome was little different: the state was Africanised but it was still imperious, greedy and coercive.

I discuss below how Africans were also clients and citizens but I want here to show how they also continued simultaneously to be subjects, which they are still today. Shorn of its historical garb, the main characteristics of subjecthood are the combination of dependence, arbitrariness and violence that is conveyed in the relation to the political master(s). Although subjects were historically under the nominal protection of their lords, that protection was at the discretion of the masters, who could withdraw it virtually at will. In Europe, the move away from subjection was the result of the gradual economic and political emancipation of the powerless: freedom was not granted; it was fought for. Processes of political change ensured that, over time, the subjects found better and more efficient means of forcing upon the powerful some form of accountability, if need be by violent means. In the end, subjecthood was abolished by the subjects themselves.

The same did not happen in post-colonial Africa. Having entrusted their future to their nationalist liberators, ordinary men and women came to realise that they had effectively mortgaged that future to 'modern' elites whom they could scarcely reach, let alone control. Or, rather, the only way they could connect with them was by means of clientelism, as I discuss below. This evolution from colonial to post-colonial subjecthood had two powerful effects. The first was the gradual disenchantment with 'modern' politics, by which I mean the realisation that it would not deliver on the promises of political emancipation that had been adumbrated by nationalism. It also meant that the trust Africans had placed in the relatively efficient working of the state, which they had experienced in colonial times, slowly began to dissipate. The second was that, as a result, Africans sought out other avenues for expressing political opinion and securing political protection. This brought about a paradoxical state of affairs, which I have dubbed political Africanisation elsewhere − that is, the mutation of 'traditional' politics to suit the new circumstances of the post-colonial situation.[3]

Therefore, there emerged in post-colonial Africa a new, 'modern', form of subjecthood, in which the populace found itself again bound to their political masters in a situation not just of inequality but also of powerlessness. Not only did the politicians fail properly to represent the ordinary men and women who had supported their nationalist campaign, they also appeared increasingly immune to the formal accountability mechanisms enshrined in the new constitutions. This new type of subjection was made concrete in the single-party political system rapidly put in place after independence. Justified as the necessary unifying expression of the nation-in-the-making, the one-party state placed ordinary people in the hands of the *apparatchiki* − who behaved more or less honourably but who applied a type of political control that could not readily be challenged. It had to be worked with: by-passed, undermined or subverted in other ways. In

---

3. Chabal, 1994: ch. 12.

practice, the combination of 'modern' political state and 'traditional' channels to the political elite resulted in a dispensation, clientelism, which drew as much from pre-colonial 'traditions' as from the requirements of post-colonial subjecthood.

CLIENT

Post-colonial subjects, then, were also clients – or at least they aspired to being clients, since they sought to secure relations of reciprocity with the new political chiefs. To say this, however, is not to say enough and much of what has been written on clientelism in Africa obscures rather than clarifies analysis. Tackling this question seriously requires that we try to understand contemporary clientelism from a historical and cultural viewpoint – and not merely from the limiting instrumental perspective that is the hallmark of Africanist political science. But first it is useful to revisit the relations between subject and client historically. In Europe, subjects were also clients in that the nature of subjecthood was in practice indicated by the type of clientelism that tied them to their overlords. Masters had obligations towards their subjects, which obligations were specified by the nature of the patrimonial link between the two.

Concretely, then, not every subject was treated the same: some had more leeway or more opportunities than others. Clearly, the nature and durability of the patrimonial relation was not in the hands of the clients and there was no recourse against arbitrary change other than revolt or flight – neither of which was easy in feudal Europe. Nevertheless, relations of clientelism conferred upon subjects a modicum of influence over their masters, especially if collectively they possessed some economic clout – by way of the production of foodstuff, for example. I have explained why in Africa subjecthood was different and why much of that difference hinged on the nature of reciprocity between rulers and ruled in the pre-colonial period. It is where we need to start our search for the nature of clientelism in African today.

In political terms, clientelism is associated with patrimonialism, an asymmetrical relation of reciprocity in which rulers acquire and retain legitimacy in so far as they meet their clients' justifiable demands, many of which are material. This means that power rests on a well-understood system of unequal exchange, in which rulers have an advantage but within which they cannot behave in arbitrary fashion. It was in this way that they were held to account in the pre-colonial period. The condition of subject was thus mitigated by the relative power the position of client allowed. There were stark limits to chiefly rule. Chiefs were selected rather than hereditary. They were liable to be replaced, deposed or even killed if they breached the boundaries of their legitimacy or failed to live up to their responsibilities. Chiefs lived with their subjects and were no more than *primus inter pares*, fully exposed to the winds of contingencies and the discontent of the populace.

Relations of clientelism were legitimate in so far as they offered the type and level of socio-political protection deemed necessary by those who lived under the chiefs' jurisdiction. But there is more. Patrimonialism was also sanctioned by the religion and culture of the time, of which it was a concrete political expression. It was thus bound by the politics of being, belonging and believing discussed above. There was an organic link between social organisation, norms and ethics that ensured patrimonialism conformed to the morality and rationality of acceptable political behaviour. It was rooted in a very direct and palpable way of life shared between rulers and ruled, who lived cheek by jowl. Whether chiefs also possessed religious powers or relied on local 'priests', their temporal authority was intimately linked to divine sanction. Politics and religion were of the same realm.

Colonial rule battered this link between power and authority but it did not sever it altogether; it distorted it greatly, sometimes to the point of emptying it of moral value. Relegated to a subaltern role within the colonial dispensation, 'traditional' patrimonialism was reshaped by the twin processes of economic change and political fiat.

The colonial overlords tolerated and exploited what they called customary law in so far as it served their administration. They allowed 'traditional' authorities continued oversight of socio-economic matters that did not impinge on the colonial economy or on colonial control. Indeed, they positively welcomed the chiefs' micro-management of local issues so long as it did not threaten colonial rule. Only where 'traditional' authorities collided against colonial interest did they interfere directly. When the Ashanti rulers became obstructive to the colonial enterprise, they had to be defeated. However, afterwards, the British were able to endorse again a now domesticated indigenous system of political authority.

Yet, the effect of colonial rule on the nexus of power and authority subsumed under the label of 'customary law' was insidiously subtle. Because power clearly rested in the colonial state, regardless of local political arrangements, the nature of clientelism had also shifted. The chiefs themselves had now become colonial clients, as was demonstrated by the fact that most of them were on the state payroll. From sitting at the apex of the local system of authority, they had become the intermediaries between colonial rulers and colonial subjects. This had two long-lasting consequences. They became accountable to their paymasters, even if they sought to maintain a properly sanctioned relation of reciprocity with their people. Second, the link between temporal and sacred authority was severely tested when not breached entirely. And it is this second factor, usually overlooked by political scientists, which matters most for what happened after independence.

The more local rulers were forced to act as colonial adjuncts, the more they lost legitimacy. Of course, appointed colonial chiefs never had much legitimacy in the first place. But even those who were recognised as rightful saw their authority eroded over time. When the gap between their action as colonially sanctioned chief and the ethical foundation on which their position rested became too wide, the moral integument of their rulership began to dissipate. Power and authority separated. Their behaviour became ethically dubious.

Because there were in all African societies religious leaders who continued to sanction the moral limits of political action, chiefs could be 'excommunicated' and thus lose all authority. Yet even where that did not happen, the growing duality between temporal and religious authority created a tension, which contributed to a fateful disjunction within the locality between power and legitimacy.

Since chiefs had access to resources, they continued to command clients. Therefore, on the surface clientelism remained as it ever was in pre-colonial times. In fact, it had mutated drastically. The patrimonial quality of chieftaincy no longer rested on the legitimacy conferred upon it by the ties of reciprocity that bound leaders and followers. It came increasingly to depend on the chiefs' capacity to distribute resources to clients. This change in the nature of patrimonialism, this move towards starker forms of patronage, had a decisive impact on the texture of accountability. Chiefs, who were now primarily accountable to the colonial state, lost their authority. They were merely the disbursers of clientelistic favours, no longer the keepers of the socio-political order. The result was a thinning of the patrimonial relation and the gradual emergence of a non-accountable form of clientelism – that is, a clientelism narrowed to the strictly instrumental, increasingly divorced from the moral and ethical dimensions of pre-colonial rulership.

This dissociation between the instrumental and the moral was aggravated by the nationalist 'revolution', which further discredited the 'traditional' system of authority and gave power to the non- or anti-traditional politicians. This 'modern' elite commonly sought to reduce, when not to obliterate, 'traditional' authority in three ways. First, it put in place a 'modern' political order that had little, or no, place for chiefly power. Second, it forced the chiefs to pay even greater allegiance to the state than the colonial masters had demanded. Third, it commuted the clientelistic relation from the 'traditional' to the 'modern' sector: the holders of state power, not the chiefs, would now command the clientelistic resources.

Paradoxically, as we shall see, the removal of patronage from chiefly hands did away with the tension between temporal and moral authority that had afflicted their rule in the colonial period. The chiefs could, and did, recover a measure of moral authority, which in due course placed them on a collision course with the post-colonial state. That in the long run the state had to come to terms with the legitimacy of chiefly authority is not the least interesting aspect of the contest between 'modern' and 'traditional' which has taken place since independence. Today, chiefs in Africa probably have more clout than they had ten years after independence.

What matters most for the interpretation of post-colonial politics is the fact that decolonisation saw the de facto institutionalisation of a relation of instrumental clientelism between political master and populace. This shift in the 'traditions' of patrimonialism was the combined result of the colonial erosion of chiefly authority and the need felt by the 'modern' political elites to seek patrimonial legitimation by means of clientelism. This meant that the clientelistic relation had become divorced from its moral attributes and now focused solely on the need for politicians to placate as large a clientele as they could muster. The fact that this form of instrumental patrimonialism could be justified on the grounds of the *letter* of the 'traditional' morality of reciprocity did not obscure the fact that the *spirit* of such morality had been left behind or simply perverted.

CITIZEN

The emphasis so far in this chapter on how Africans are both subjects and clients should not detract from the very obvious point that since independence they have also been citizens. Before I proceed with my analysis of what it has meant to be a citizen in the postcolony, I want to make it plain that a main argument of this chapter is that Africans (as others elsewhere in the world) are at one and the same time subject, client and citizen. Not only do they inhabit, admittedly in unequal measure depending on local circumstances, all three political spheres but the very specificity of their contemporary condition is that the three interact in ways that it is important to conceptualise if one is to understand post-colonial politics on the continent.

On the question of citizenship, political science offers clear guidance, derived from the Western experience, and it is from such notions that we ought to start. As ever, I shall eschew definitional orthodoxy and favour instead a broad notion that encapsulates the essence of that political affiliation. But first a caveat: although there is much talk of citizenship in Africa, there is too little acknowledgement of the historical roots of that concept. Indeed, it is difficult to conceive of citizenship outside of the context of a political system (whatever its ideological persuasion) in which the identity, rights and obligations of the individual person are made constitutionally explicit and are juridically upheld. What this means is that both the quintessence and the reality of citizenship are inextricably bound up with a 'modern' political and judicial dispensation which affords protection to the discrete individual *qua* individual.

From a formal viewpoint, all Africans are officially citizens of a particular country. They all have the right of nationality (even if they cannot always manage to get a passport) and are all covered in principle by the protection the constitution bestows upon them. More subjectively, there is little doubt that Africans do identify, never more strongly than when football is at stake, with their country of citizenship. Whatever differences may separate individuals within a particular country, there is clearly a vibrant bond that joins them together when it comes to expressing or defending national interests. The argument that Africans are still in the throes of 'primordial' rather than national sentiments does not withstand serious examination – though the question of what 'primordial' might mean ought not so blithely to be discarded solely on account of the concept's historical trajectory. Africans are citizens indeed. However, when it comes to assessing the virtue of citizenship or, more particularly, what it means concretely in daily life, the situation is less clear.

Beyond this simple definition of political identity, therefore, there are a number of issues that cloud the reality of citizenship and in practice limit its reach. The first, which is becoming increasingly salient today, has to do with the doubts expressed by sundry governments about the validity of the national origins of some of their citizens, even if settled in the country since independence. As we've seen in the previous chapter on belonging, there are now in Africa increasingly numerous cases where the criteria of citizenship are being altered. In what was originally a manoeuvre to exclude rivals, politicians have tampered with the constitutional definition of nationality in ways that have been highly problematic, since many Africans have complicated and diverse backgrounds that do not tailor with the exigencies of present national borders. This has disenfranchised significant numbers and has produced a climate of uncertainty, which is detrimental to the consolidation of a sense of national unity and excites xenophobic nationalism.

Another problem is tied to the numerous conflicts that have broken out in the last twenty years, many of which have revived ancient fears about certain groups and created exclusive divisions where none existed previously. If the most notorious such example is that of eastern Zaire/DRC – where long-established Hutu and Tutsi communities have been deemed un-Congolese because of recent events in Rwanda and because of Rwandan involvement beyond its borders – there are many other cases of contingent disenfranchisement arising out of violence and war. Equally, the move in Ethiopia to an ethnically based federal system has facilitated the casting of aspersions and the accusations of disloyalty against those groups (e.g. Somali, Oromo) that are deemed by the government to have dubious commitment to the nation. Whatever the causes of such political exclusions, the arbitrary removal of citizenship from people who had long assumed it was theirs has undermined that supposedly hallowed form of political affiliation and contributed to the unravelling of the nation.

The third issue relates to those groups who never fully accepted their incorporation into a particular national entity (for instance, the southerners in Sudan or the Tuaregs in Niger) or who now feel that, for political reasons, they no longer really belong to their country of citizenship (e.g. the anglophone provinces of Cameroon). Here, it is the individuals from these groups who entertain a very guarded relation with the national state, convinced as they are that their inclusion in that country was against their interests. For them, citizenship is precarious and fails to offer either the rights or the protection to which they aspire. In turn, they are viewed with suspicion by their own government, which easily suspects them of being real or crypto secessionists. Such suspicion fuels xenophobia and, often, violence. In this case, too, citizenship is far from being obvious or uncontested; it is but an artificial construct that does not meet the groups' sense of self-identity and is still not settled, decades after independence.

This first cluster of problems with present notions of citizenship is not one that is confined to Africa. Elsewhere, too, there are examples of the lack of fit between the official criteria of nationality and the realities on the ground. In point of fact, given the wholly artificial nature of colonial frontiers in Africa and the number of groupings that were split by these borders at independence, it is remarkable that there are so few such doubts expressed about citizenship. However, continued violence and conflict on the continent would certainly aggravate the situation considerably.

The second cluster, which touches on the significance for citizenship of institutional weakness, is also common outside Africa. Nevertheless, considering the present condition of the continent, it is in that part of the world that these problems are most acute. In a nutshell, the less secure and effective national institutions are, the weaker citizenship effectively becomes. Furthermore, the erosion of citizenship that such institutional weakness brings about can be swift and drastic, undoing decades of stability. The reconstruction of a sense of citizenship is bound to be more difficult than its dissolution. The point here is that citizenship is not made of stone, secure once it has been achieved. It is fragile and, as long as it has not survived intact the chaos and violence of the African postcolony,[4] it cannot be assumed that it will endure unchanged. Indeed, some scholars are dubious about the long-term survival of nation-states on the continent.[5]

Although ostensibly it is now central to the political identity of the overwhelming majority of Africans, there are a number of processes undermining this sense of belonging and in some instances damaging it fatally. Of these, some are *contingent*, some are *structural* and some are *cultural*. I've touched above on some of the contingent events that can affect citizenship and turn long-established citizens into stateless refugees. Equally, the constant denigration of some groups within a polity can unleash major tremors that will shake national boundaries and national identities long after the fact. At best, it will take a generation before the peoples who formally belong to Rwanda feel they are citizens of the same country again. However, if contingent factors can be severely disruptive, they are perhaps less lethal in the long run than the structural or cultural ones.

By *structural* elements, I mean the evolution of national institutions in ways that undermine the very concept of citizenship – and thereby lead, even if unwittingly, to the resurgent saliency of earlier notions of identity, many of which rooted in the pre-colonial period. These structural factors fall into two broad categories: those that define a sense of citizenship that is congruent with the national boundaries as they were drawn at independence, regardless of their artificiality; and those that uphold the reality of citizenship in the face of the contingent events that threaten its existence. In turn, these factors are affected by the institutional quality of politics and the socio-economic conditions in which people live. I discuss them in turn.

4. Mbembe, 2000.
5. Herbst, 2000.

Clearly, the robustness of citizenship is dependent on the continued commitment of governments to a shared sense of nationality. Where this weakens or dissipates, there is a great risk that ordinary people will resort to other means of securing identity and protection – of which clientelism and ethnicity are the most common. The dereliction of institutions, which is marked by their increasingly arbitrary operation, also leads to disenchantment with a form of affiliation that is not meaningful in practice. If Africans have long been accustomed to bribe their way for a passport, they take exception to the random denial of their rights as citizens by an ineffective, discriminatory or downright dishonest bureaucracy. Those who cannot get papers proceed on their long march without them. As they seek fortune elsewhere, they lose any real sense of citizenship and they cling to an identity that becomes less national and more translocal. In cases where institutions have ceased functioning altogether, citizenship becomes virtual – no less real in terms of football but singularly less relevant otherwise.

Similarly, the socio-economic health of a country has a bearing on the quality of citizenship. Even if by now, so many decades after independence, Africans do adhere strongly to one national identity, the nature of that adhesion is coloured by the conditions of their existence. Poverty and destitution test the sense of commitment to the very notion of nationality. Citizenship is not just defined by the country to which one belongs but perhaps more significantly by the ways one is devoted to that country *qua* homeland. If few Africans would envisage formally switching nationality, those whose socio-economic circumstances are unsatisfactory feel that their status as citizen is less and less relevant to the realities of their lives. In so far as people believe that the state – in effect the institutional embodiment of the nation – has a duty of care towards them, the thinning of the state's efficacy undermines the meaning of citizenship.

The dissolving of a sense of citizenship, if and when it occurs, brings into play a number of *cultural* factors, some of which are inimical to the consolidation of the nation-state. Where individuals or groups become convinced that their national identity is politically or materially irrelevant to their daily lives, they quite naturally seek solutions elsewhere. Since, as I have explained, the tenor of identity in Africa is primarily communal, it is in that direction that people turn for succour. Whether this translates into ethnic claims, even irredentism, or whether it materialises in other demands, the upshot is recourse to what is seen by Africanist political science merely as 'traditional' forms of identity. However, what takes place is more complex. People are not primarily looking backward to a golden age before the nation-state. They are looking beyond the nation-state, which has failed them, to new forms of identity that will be more profitable. Their claims may appear parochial but are in fact 'modern' and they engender political dynamics likely to affect both the nature and the viability of the nation-state in Africa.

The other major direction in which Africans turn is the spiritual. Again, religion in itself is not in direct competition with citizenship: a newly converted Christian is not going to seek another nationality. Nevertheless, an engagement with matters of faith, whether 'traditional' or 'modern', does affect the reality of citizenship as it is experienced in everyday life. In this respect, the most important shift has been the enormous sweep of Pentecostalism in Africa. By far the fastest growing religion on the continent, it has had a strong influence on its adherents' sense of identity and on their behaviour. Pentecostalism is subversive in many different ways, some of which are corrosive of citizenship. Not only does it strongly reject 'traditional' beliefs, it also advocates a decidedly 'modern' and individualist notion of (economic and political) agency – of which personal self-improvement and internationalism are perhaps the two most significant – which often conflicts with the prevailing ethos. Worthy as they may appear to the American churches that sponsor Pentecostalism, these priorities are disruptive of received notions of identity, reciprocity and even nationality. In ways that are not always discernible today, they could pose a greater challenge to the African polity than is presently envisaged.

Having outlined how Africans are simultaneously subjects, clients and citizens, I now want to discuss how this matters for contemporary politics. In the first place, it means that those analysts who limit their remarks to one, or even two, of the three are likely to miss a large part of the picture. This is particularly true of observers who see in Africa only emaciated subjects, irredeemable clients or emancipated citizens. The reality is more messy, even more than is conveyed by these three categories, since how they are interpreted by individuals and groups depends on the local factors outlined in the first three chapters. In other words, what it means in practice to be subject, client or citizen is unlikely to be similar in all parts of a country. The ways in which it is dissimilar is likely to have an influence on how local people interpret the role of politicians, of 'traditional' authorities and more generally of the institutions of the state. For instance, Kikuyus and Maasais do have different notions of political *partaking*, and this for good historical and cultural grounds to which heed ought to be paid when discussing Kenyan post-colonial politics. The former identify themselves in terms of relation to land; the latter in terms of cattle – which means they interpret their place as citizens in distinct fashion.

Second, the more interesting questions about political participation in Africa are those that seek to elucidate the ways in which these three different forms of political identity overlap and interact. It is indeed one of the great limitations of political science that it seeks so insistently to separate out these various categories, as though it were compelled by some 'scientific' necessity to slot human beings into one or the other. However necessary it is analytically to simplify, it is no less important to try to find ways of reflecting reality as it actually is. The problem with Africanist scholarship is not so much that it is wrong-headed but that it is content to limit the reach of interpretation to that which suits familiar (largely Western) categories of analysis. But it is in the uncovered nuances of life, in the inconsistencies of individual and group behaviour, that a more enlightening vision of events and processes is to be found. There are no pristine subjects, clients or citizens but only people who are haphazardly all three.

Indeed, what marks out the African postcolony is this highly chaotic and broken-up reality in which the extremes cohabit in strange configurations. In the course of a single day, individuals can be subject, client and citizen depending on what happens to them. For instance, most African states treat their citizens like subjects in their day-to-day dealings with them: officials, police, party functionaries, and so on, are wont to exercise arbitrary rule over those they can cow – like those who are not in a position to resist the unwarranted demand upon them, say, at a police roadblock. Violence of a kind permeates all aspects of the relations between state and populace and it is a matter of happenstance how often individuals have to endure such abuse. Of course, some people suffer arbitrary rule more than others but my point is simply that hardly anyone escapes that condition at some stage in their life.

At the same time, and it is one of the benefits of regular elections, most people in Africa are treated like citizens when called upon to vote. Politicians in Africa have certainly been acutely aware of the need to court their peoples as fully entitled members of the polity. What is variable is the extent to which they do so by means of full or only partial clientelistic means. On this question, it is generally assumed that multiparty elections are more 'democratic', whereas what such electoral competition frequently induces is a heightened recourse to 'traditional' forms of political mobilisation that rest firmly on clientelistic grounds. Paradoxically, at least for those who view competitive democracy as the blueprint for political modernisation, the one-party state actually forced politicians to spread more widely their clientelistic net. Success depended on broad, rather than narrowly communal, appeal. The upshot might have been more patrimonial but at least it was less brutally ethnic – compare Kenya under Kenyatta, Arap Moi and Kibaki.

Equally, it is assumed that clientelism is incompatible with citizenship – which might be true within a narrow Western interpretation.

Yet, this is not so straightforward. As we have seen, clientelism rests on long-established relations of reciprocity, which include some (admittedly 'traditional' or informal) forms of political accountability. Patrons do have obligations towards their clients. So that in some, but obviously not in all, instances of clientelism, what the patrons provide can be seen as the necessities of citizenship – belonging and protection. In such cases, it can be argued that there is a de facto recognition of a concept of citizenship that binds both patrons and clients within a single political dispensation. It is true that this form of citizenship does not tally with the constitution and that the clientelistic nature of such a relation of dependence may interfere with the workings of the polity as a whole. Yet, where citizenship is devoid of practical use, clientelism may 'work'.

Therefore, what is wrong with much Africanist political theory is the assumption that what is best in the West is *ipso facto* best for Africa. This might be true in the sense that a functioning liberal-democratic order would benefit Africa if it could be imported so as to work fully formed. But since this has not happened, what is left for political analysts is to try to understand how Africans make do in less than agreeable conditions. It is undoubtedly the case that most Africans are unhappy with the form of political participation they are offered in the postcolony. It is equally true that none would reject a type of citizenship that enabled them to compel their governments to devote their energies to the improvement of the general well-being. However, this is not the choice they face. For them, therefore, political *partaking* is often the least bad combination of subject, client and citizen they can contrive in the circumstances.

FIVE

The politics of striving

If the previous chapter sought to understand what might be called the civic nature of political participation from the ground up, this one centres on the politics of economic activity, also from the perspective of ordinary people. Because the chapter's angle – the emphasis on 'striving' – may appear odd, I need to explain what I am trying to do. For good reasons, most economists would want to explain Africa's predicament – lack of development and poverty – in terms of the continent's place in the world economy. Indeed, there is a vast literature on the international dimensions of African economies, which is valuable, and much of what I say, in this chapter and in the next one, will draw on the analysis of the international dimensions of Africa's economies.

However, here I want to eschew the usual attempt to survey the continent's political economy from a global standpoint and approach the question from the perspective of individuals and groups, who engage in economic activities as and when they can. How do people face up to the need to work? What does it mean to them? How do they strive to secure a decent life and, when possible, to improve their condition? Again, I consider these questions from a somewhat unusual angle in that I do not primarily seek to present sociological findings. I want instead to try to reinterpret the significance of the relation between work and politics. In order to do so, I return to questions that are often taken for granted in Africanist political science.

In this respect, the two dominant assumptions in economic theory today are that (1) there is a correlation between economic activity and some form of class development; and (2) that left to their own devices, individuals become strong actors on the market and market forces will drive development. The first derives from an understanding of the relation between labour and social differentiation that issues from a near-universal (Marxian) view of the link between economic and political change. Here the expectation is that individuals come to behave politically in consonance with their place in the productive system. The second is the foundation of the current development orthodoxy. If they could, ordinary Africans would seize the opportunities available in the (domestic and international) market and contribute in this way to economic growth. Thus, aid policy and economic conditionalities should be geared to 'freeing' the economy in Africa from its 'traditional' (meaning clientelistic) shackles.

On the whole, these are assumptions shared by Africanist political scientists. Even those who oppose globalisation, who see in the world market the cause of Africa's underdevelopment and who advocate some kind of more redistributive political economy, subscribe, if a contrario, to these suppositions. My argument is that such approaches – pro or contra world market economics – miss out on the type of evidence that is critical to the understanding of the relationship between work and politics. By reducing economic discussion to what is on the agenda of economists, whether African or outsiders, one may easily fail to consider other important factors that affect people in their day-to-day lives – factors which impinge very greatly on the prospects for economic development. If, to take but one example, wealth accumulated today in an African country like Nigeria is, as prima facie seems the case, disbursed primarily for the assertion of social standing, then it is not going to be invested according to the capitalist logic that is supposed to lie at the heart of economic growth.

Instead of assuming that people work in certain ways to certain ends, I want to investigate how what they actually do comes together to shape what is called the economy. Although governments (generally) attempt to direct people's activities into a more nationally productive way, the reality for most Africans is the overwhelming dominance of what economists call the informal sector. The label itself betrays the difficulty they face in understanding the systemic nature of this economic activity, which is only informal in that it cannot be taxed. But in a situation where most of the economy is informal it ought to be seen as the real economy, the study of which should be the starting point of any attempt to understand how people earn what they need in order to live. Indeed, a focus on the informal immediately forces us to ask questions about work in a different way.

In this chapter, I approach the question of the economy from three different angles: *labour*, *trade* and *rent*. What I intend to cover here is what *labour* means and how that influences how people work or fail to work. I then look at the links between such notions and the overwhelming importance of *trade* in Africa. Finally, I assess why it is that African economies are largely based on *rent* – that is, the search for income that can obviate the need to generate resources internally. Although I do not think there are simple causal links between these three aspects of the question, I believe there are connections which can help to explain the present economic situation in Africa and cast some useful light on contemporary African politics.

LABOUR

If all economists would agree that the basis of the economy is labour, most of them make assumptions which need to be discussed. Among those that we should reconsider are the nature of labour and the ends to which it is put. On the first, the presumption is that people work, if not to fulfil a need at least because they want to better their conditions. But is this always the case? Or, to put it another way, do people always labour within a future-oriented perspective? On the second, the theory is that work is geared to instrumental ends that are essentially driven by the need to accumulate. But how true is this in an environment that may prize stability over change? These questions must be examined, rather than wished away. By now it is fairly obvious that the distinction between formal and informal economies makes little sense in Africa, other than as code words for certain types of activities. However, there is still reluctance to rethink the concept of labour.

Perhaps we should reconsider the distinction between formal and informal labour in different ways. The former refers to that part of work which belongs to the formal economy of salaries, taxes, investment and accumulation. The latter encompasses the work that goes into the non-formal economy, most of which consists in buying and selling in small quantities or offering limited services on an ad hoc basis. The main differences between the two types of labour are not so much the effort deployed, the returns on hours worked or even the sums involved, but rather the perspective within which these activities take place.

Formal labour, which is limited in contemporary Africa, is of two sorts: state and private-sector employment. The first is generally deficient in that civil servants are not paid enough, when they are paid at all. They cannot aspire to a professional and personal life in keeping with their expectations and that would help them commit themselves wholly to their employment within the institutions in which they work. Therefore, they often participate in the informal economy, at the expense of their official duties. And those who can, leave state service to take employment in the foreign-funded NGO sector, where salaries are much higher and paid regularly.

The formal private sector is itself divided between foreign and domestic firms. Of these, only foreign companies are in a position to offer conditions of service, and demand conditions of work, that approximate those found in non-African countries. Here, formal labour is clearly at work. In the domestic sector, uncertainty is much greater because of a number of economic, social and political factors which conspire to reduce the efficiency of these businesses. The economic issues have to do with the difficulty of competing in terms of finance, investment and management with foreign businesses. The social issues concern the necessity felt by domestic businessmen to play their part in the economy of reciprocity to which they belong, which reduces both the capacity to accumulate and the ability to manage. The political questions boil down to the ubiquitous attempts by those in power to extract rent from businesses by means of measures that can make life very difficult for entrepreneurs.

There are three important points about this division between formal and informal which matter for African political economies. The first is that informal economic activities do not lend themselves to long-term productive investment unless they can be transformed into recognisable formal businesses. The second is that most formal activities involve informal factors, by way of what has sometimes been called the 'economy of affection',[1] which inevitably reduces the capacity and competitiveness of the businesses concerned. The third is that most economic actors are involved in both formal and informal activities, making for a precarious existence, which again militates against investment and economic stability.

The constant juxtaposition of formal and informal makes for remarkable flexibility and resilience, as is every day evidenced by the ingenuity with which Africans navigate the treacherous economic waters on which they are cast. However, it tends to produce an economy of the here and now, of immediate results and success, of a display and sharing of wealth, which is inimical to the continuity in activities needed for investment or economic growth. Within such an economic environment, labour is perceived differently from the way in which it is conceptualised in standard economic theory. Economic

---

1. Hydén, 1980.

actors are not necessarily looking to the most economically rewarding or promising activity but to that which is likely to provide greatest security over the longest possible time frame. Since the returns on labour in the formal sector are both limited and precarious, they offer little security except for a tiny business elite.

Paradoxically, therefore, the informal sector is a necessary corollary to the formal economy. The formal economy could not operate without the informal economy, and there is a mutually beneficial symbiosis between the two. This is significant politically. Politicians are in a perilous business, as they well know, and they expend considerable energy in securing for themselves informal economic advantages. This means they strengthen, and in that sense legitimate, the informal sector and the use of informal labour. By investing in the informal sector, they seek personal and immediate rewards from the negotiation of political protection, or patronage. Formal activities that are not so well protected or favoured by the political elites find themselves in an insecure position.

What might be called the informalisation of the economy, and hence of labour, is reinforced by two further processes at work. One is that, because African economies are structurally weak, there is little correlation between education and employment. Whilst it is true that a minority of graduates can aspire to work as civil servants or other professional jobs, the numbers are small and the rewards paltry. The vast majority of young people cannot find employment, let alone employment that would match their qualifications. The upshot is that education bestows no real right to labour and that finding work is more likely the result of informal factors – that is, patronage. Indeed, the best way of finding employment – other than scraping a living in petty trade on the streets – is to rely on the economy of obligation or the networks of reciprocity that can be tapped.

The second is that, with some exceptions, the informal economy has become central to the operation of the formal – not just in the sense described above – but in terms of the fact that the very operation of formal activities is predicated upon the deployment of informal sanction. This includes the granting of business licences, the availability of bank loans, the provision of the necessary infrastructural inputs (energy, communications), foreign exchange availability, export permits, and so on. Even in the case of foreign-owned and -operated companies, such informal constraints apply and they effectively act either as barriers to entry or as hidden tax.

These conditions, therefore, have a direct impact on the meaning of labour in Africa, which largely invalidates the standard political economy theory used by Africanist political scientists. This is a vast subject and I will stress only a few aspects which may help explain the apparent 'irrationality' (from a Western point of view) of African economic actors. As we have seen, with few exceptions the bulk of the African population is active in the informal sector and operates according the rules of the informal economy. Because of the precarious nature of that sector, the priority is the maximisation of security rather than income and the time frame is the present rather than the future. Furthermore, labour depends on the economy of reciprocity rather than on the market per se. Or, rather, the market operates within the constraints of the economy of obligation. Ultimately, economic efficiency (in the Western sense) is secondary to the more immediate need to secure resources, here and now. Local economic rationality requires the cultivation of 'traditional' networks and values, which economists habitually see as impediments to the development of a market economy.

In such circumstances, people's labour is best invested in cultivating the conditions that will sustain the informal economy on which they depend. This involves committing substantial time and resources to ostensibly non-economic activities. For example, it may be more important for some people to propitiate the dead in the village, or to support financially a vast array of distant relatives, than to invest the profits from a shop in town into expanding their business. Or it may make more sense not to behave according to economic 'rationality' at all. For instance, it may be better to curtail one's economic activities at a level that is deemed modest rather than to grow to a size that appears 'affluent' – for that would trigger disproportionately larger demands from kin and dependants, which would leave the business even more precariously balanced financially. Or finally, it may be rational to work for nothing, if it secures the protection of a powerful godfather who can provide resources and security otherwise unavailable.

Clearly, such circumstances have a bearing on politics. Where labour is endowed with such a vast assortment of meanings, many of which relate to 'traditional' relations of power, there develops a political economy that bears little relation to the theory of the market. If politicians depend on the informal economy, they also possess the means to influence its viability. Therefore, labour is also to be invested in cultivating the right politicians and in supporting the policies they want enforced. At one extreme, this may translate into joining the youth militias politicians increasingly deploy to secure dominance (especially where young males have virtually no prospect of employment). More generally, it may involve devoting time and effort supporting politicians and helping secure their tenure of power. Here, multiparty polls have vastly increased the need for politicians to deploy armies of 'workers', whose labour must somehow be rewarded if they are to ensure re-election.

TRADE

The central role of the informal in the workings of African economies helps to explain why on the continent trade is so widespread. Other than agricultural production for food, the bulk of Africa's economic activities are concerned with commerce – formal or informal, legal or illegal – which essentially boils down to the exchange of goods for money. That such is the case is not in dispute, so the question is why. Why the predominance of trade even when conditions (e.g. labour and investors) exist for the transformation of raw material (e.g. bauxite, cotton, coffee) into intermediate goods with more added value? This is an especially important question since economic theory asserts, and the experience of (among others) East Asian countries confirms, that (1) greater profit is made from the transformation of primary products than from their mere export and (2) economic development hinges on moving away from the export of primary products to the production of manufactured commodities.

Clearly, there are a large number of factors that come into play. They range from the historical – Africa was made dependent on world trade by colonial exploitation – to the structural – Africa has not developed the infrastructure to make such production possible. All these are significant and they all deserve attention. But since these areas are well covered in the literature, I will only refer to them when they relate to my main area of concern, which has to do with the logic of those who engage in trade as seen from their point of view. This is not to deny that such logic may well also be conditioned by the bigger (international and domestic) economic picture but only to say that I want to understand the political implications of the primacy of trade from the ground up.

My argument is, first, that there are specific historical, social, political and cultural reasons why trade is so central and, second, that there are logical connections between these factors that help to explain the present situation.

The case for trade liberalisation is that, if Africa derived greater benefits from its current exports, it could more easily invest into economically productive activities, which in turn would favour development. The assumption, therefore, is that greater revenues from trade would provide the means to effect structural changes in the economy – changes towards the production of manufactured goods that are more profitable. But this is a big assumption, not just because Africa is not (or has hitherto not been) in a position to evolve the human and infrastructural resources that are required but also because present policies do not lead in that direction. It may well be, then, that it is better to approach the question of the pre-eminence of trade in African economies within a broader perspective.

I have explained how the nature of labour was intimately connected with the importance of the informal economy and how
the informal economy rested on the economy of obligation. This
economy of obligation is in turn linked to the 'traditional' socio-
cultural framework of what I've called the political economy of
reciprocity. Let us now see how trade fitted historically into this social
matrix. I would like to highlight here the interaction between three
types of factors: *historical, cultural* and *political*. The first is linked to
the complexion of African economies from the pre-colonial period;
the second examines the importance of beliefs, norms and values
for economic activities; the third touches on the role of politics in
the economy in today's Africa.

Historically, Africa has been a land of movement, migration and
above all commerce. Far from the image of a continent frozen in
time before the colonial period, Africa was always involved in local
and long-distance trade, which linked some of the more remote
areas in the interior to markets across the Sahara or beyond the
seas. The expansion of certain peoples across the continent and the
spread of the cultivation of certain crops are intimately linked to
the prevalence of trade. Other than some remote groups (Pygmies
in central Africa or San in southern Africa), all other communities
engaged in long-distance commercial relations. There were in pre-
colonial Africa numerous cities and markets, which made trading
possible on a vast scale across huge spans. The slave trade itself was
not just the inhuman exploitation by Europeans of those they treated
like chattel but also the result of the fact that many African rulers
engaged in the traffic of human beings, often on a massive scale.
Commerce was the bulwark of the economy, and if humans could
be traded profitably, they were.

The early contacts with Europe comforted the Africans with the
impression that the Europeans were only the latest in a long line of
outsiders who came to trade. For several centuries, the relations between the two were built on mutually beneficial commerce. During
that period there was no indication in Africa that Europeans were

interested in anything other than the exchange of goods, including people. It was the nineteenth-century transformation in the political economy of the main European countries that brought about a sudden and cataclysmic change for the Africans: trade was no longer enough; the imperialists now needed to own the continent's resources and redirect local human energy into more 'profitable' labour. There was thus a complete rupture not just in the relations between Africans and Europeans but also in the nature of economic exchange.

This had enormous consequences for Africa. Here, I want to stress how that divorce between Africa's historical economy of trade and the realities of an increasingly powerful world market impinged on the behaviour of Africa's main economic actors. Since the colonial economy was geared to servicing the needs of the imperial powers, Africans adapted to it in several ways. The elite joined the civil service and its ancillary public administration. Those who could do so went into export agriculture; others provided food to the cities. Many worked for industry: in mining, in factories or in transport. Yet others were employed, or coerced, into the construction industry, building cities, houses, roads, bridges and railways. Although some were self-employed, particularly in agriculture and transport, most were dependent on employment offered or generated by the colonial economy. During that period, domestic and international trade patterns were dictated by the needs of the colonial economy. Often (wholesale but also retail) commerce was taken over by foreigners: Indians or Lebanese. The upshot was that, with the exception of a few successful entrepreneurs, Africans were left with the less profitable sectors of the colonial economy and the informal sector.

Crucially, the colonial period rarely brought about the establishment of sustainable national economies since most countries were geared to the export of their primary and material resources. The post-colonial period inevitably resulted in a hybrid economy, a leftover from the colonial one. Although complex in its detail, the evolution since independence has witnessed the gradual collapse of the industrial sector; the continued reliance on the export of primary products; the emergence of a sizable, sometimes dominant, informal economy of trade – some of which in illegal goods or illicit substances; and, finally, an increasing dependence on aid transfers. I will discuss the question of transfers below. Here I want to show how the evolution of the post-colonial economy has been in the direction of the reconsolidation of (formal or informal) trade. Given the hazardous nature of such trade and the instability of prices on the world market, this has been a poor foundation upon which to base a programme of economic development.

This focus on trade was perhaps not entirely coincidental since it has built on important cultural factors, which favour a political economy of exchange and rely on well-established 'traditional' networks that facilitate commerce. Of course, Africans are not the only ones to have had long-standing trading networks, as I will discuss in the next chapter. Indians, Chinese and Arabs also have a centuries-old history of international commerce. So, the question is not whether cultural factors only came into play in respect of Africa but how they have affected all communities involved in trade, in Africa as elsewhere. Some of these factors are common; others are specific. More importantly, the question is why other parts of the world moved from trade to manufacture whilst this has not happened in Africa. This is a fundamental issue, which scores of economists have discussed for decades, and I do not pretend I can provide a simple answer single-handedly. I simply want to trace the links between history, culture and economy.

My argument is that in Africa the weight of colonial history reinforced strong tendencies in indigenous societies to privilege commerce over manufacture. Clearly, most nationalist leaders at independence had a vision of a rapidly modernising Africa that would move the economy from trade into the industrial age, which was deemed the only path to development. For those governments that leaned in a socialist direction, the Soviet or Chinese experiences provided a possible model. For the others, it was the countries of

Western Europe after the Second World War that inspired confidence in state planning and industrialisation. However, the reality of what happened is that politicians seemed to have allowed, or favoured, the use of the (largely state) industrial sector for patrimonial purposes, so as to strengthen the legitimacy of their rule by diverting state resources into clientelistic networks. At the same time, the newly independent governments failed to sustain investment into the type of human resources (e.g. education, training, health) and infrastructure (transport, banking, energy and communications) required for economic development.

The standard Africanist political science explanation for this boils down to a failure of political leadership. But the question is why this happened. Whilst not denying such failure, I am interested in finding out whether there were reasons above and beyond incompetence, greed, corruption, tyranny, and so on, for such a general trend in post-colonial Africa. In point of fact, not all first-generation leaders were corrupt, incompetent or tyrannical; some were quite successful in the pursuit of economic policies that were adjudged (for a time) to be successful by the populations concerned. So what happened? Two explanations suggest themselves here. One is that, having resources to trade, it was easier to follow that course, especially since in the 1960s world market prices were high. The other, however, is that there was in Africa a long-standing predilection for trade, which fitted the expectations of all, from top to bottom.

Historically and culturally, it had always been assumed that the primary form of economic activity was exchange and that the purpose of trading was the acquisition of goods or monies for the assertion of status and the discharging of patrimonial obligations. It is this factor, entirely neglected by Africanist political science, which could provide at least part of an explanation for a type of economic behaviour that must otherwise be dismissed either as aberrant or, depending on the calibre of the politicians, as corrupt. The point, therefore, is that this continued emphasis on trade as the main pillar of the economy has deeper roots in the historical and socio-cultural fabric of African societies than is allowed for by current theories of political economy.

Within this perspective, it becomes easier to understand both why politicians went for trade and why their constituents expected they should share the benefits of such trade according to the ever-present norms of reciprocity that are at the core of the economy of obligation. At least such an explanation has the merit of taking seriously what seems to be a near-universal logic in the evolution of post-colonial African economies. If this state of affairs has been detrimental to economic development as it is usually conceived in the West or to the construction of a sustainable industrial base in Africa, it has been highly profitable for those involved in this (legal or illegal) trade. Indeed, commerce has provided the bulk of the resources that have enabled ordinary Africans to survive and it has offered immense riches to the most successful entrepreneurs – among whom politicians have been conspicuous. This could not have happened if such an economic activity had not been in harmony with the tenets of the economy of obligation outlined in the first three chapters.

Lest this argument be misconstrued, I want to offer the following caveats. First, to say that trade is so congenial to the continent is not to say that no other activity can, or will, develop. Change will undoubtedly have to take place, if only because the present dispensation leaves increasing numbers of Africans in poverty. Second, the fact that trade is so ubiquitous does not imply that it is always legitimate. Clearly, illegality and corruption are undermining the legitimacy of commerce, which again is not sustainable in the long run. Third, the business of illegality is beginning to wear thin among a population that is increasingly deprived of the bounties of clientelism. Fourth, the world community is becoming less tolerant of sharp-trade practices, which clearly fail greater and greater number of Africans. Finally, this analysis does not rest on an argument that tradition is more important in Africa. It simply points to the necessity for political science to understand how tradition matters. To neglect 'tradition' is to be ahistorical.

RENT

The consequence of the evolution of post-colonial African economies, as adumbrated so far, has been a tendency towards rent-seeking, at all levels of society. Whilst there is nothing new or particularly African about rent economies, the question is why rent-seeking has become more pronounced in that part of the world. The ostensibly straightforward, and undoubtedly most common, answer is that African politicians have been able to access rent on such a scale because they abuse power. That may be true in some instances but not every politician has behaved like the former Nigerian leader Soni Abacha, whose aim clearly was to accumulate as large a private fortune as he could muster. So, this will not do as an explanation, reassuring as it may be to some, for the simple reason that rent-seeking is too widespread and too ingrained to be brushed off as the mere misdeed of a few corrupt politicians.

On this issue, again, political science is singularly devoid of any critical angle other than the normative. It considers this state of affairs as pathological and posits from the outset that it is incompatible with development. Furthermore, it assumes that rent-seeking is the mark of 'traditional' societies and that it disappears as polities become more institutionalised and democratic. As always, this may have been true of (some at least among) Western societies as they evolved historically but it can scarcely be presumed that it is the case everywhere – even less that there is a single sequence of political development that obliterates rent-seeking in such fine manner. Certainly in the case of Africa, where by all accounts rent-seeking is becoming more, rather than less, pronounced, this assumption needs to be challenged.

Here, I want to investigate whether rent-seeking has deeper roots than is usually believed and, if it does, what this may imply for the politics of striving on the continent. Because rent is a well established form of economic activity, with many historical precedents, the question is try to make sense of the African variant of this phenomenon. What interests me is to place rent-seeking as it is currently taking place in Africa within a more specific local historical and socio-cultural context. In this respect, it seems to me that there are a number of areas worth investigating. The first is the relationship between rent and *status*. The second is the extent to which rent-seeking is *collective*. The third is the link between the construction of post-colonial nation-states and the politics of *aid* (as rent) since independence. Taken together these three elements might help to explain the prominence of rent-seeking in Africa today.

What I mean by *status* is the extent to which rent confers symbolic as well as material advantage on the beneficiary. Whilst it is almost always true that status and wealth go together, it is also frequently the case that the way in which wealth is acquired has great political significance. So, what is relevant here is how symbolically significant rent has been in African societies. There seems little doubt that king or chiefly status in pre-colonial Africa was associated with rent. The mark of political, religious and social eminence was measured by the extent to which tribute was paid by those who came under the rulers' jurisdiction. Clearly, the same was true in all feudal or quasi-feudal systems worldwide. What was more specifically African was the extent to which the size of the tribute was in itself the main mark of distinction. In other words, tribute was not merely a token of vassalage, an agreed submission to specific chiefly rule; it was also, and perhaps primarily, a gauge of the chief's eminence. The accumulation of wealth, often in the form of cattle, was worthy in and of itself – not primarily because it gave the chief added economic clout but because it was the embodiment of his greatness. Tribute, therefore, had a direct role in making manifest, in the most highly visible form, the eminence of the chief's status.

Although the accumulation of wealth was sometimes put to specific practical use, such as raising an army or buying off rivals, it was mostly of little direct economic value. Chiefs were not traders or entrepreneurs, whose own wealth, however large, could never challenge that of their rulers precisely because chiefs obtained theirs through tribute and not business. What mattered to status, therefore, was not simply to acquire wealth for its own sake but to demonstrate the ability to do so by means of tribute, or rent, which became thereby the material embodiment of symbolic status. Indeed, not only were chiefs not meant to behave like businessmen, they were expected to act as the keepers of the status attached to their rank. Tribute was central but the proceeds of rent, wealth, were not their personal property; they were attached to the position they held – a position they occupied by consent. This was true even in so-called acephalous societies since there the village head was also selected by his peers and his status also involved tribute of some kind, if on a less lavish scale.

Another consequence of this 'traditional' set-up was the obverse: namely, that chiefs and kings *expected* their wealth to be generated by rent. Not just because this was their chiefly prerogative but also because the process of receiving rent was itself a symbolic marker of their status. In other words, chiefs did not exploit their position to become rich; they became rich because of their position – which imposed on them a duty to exhibit as much substance as they could in order both to uphold their rank and to offer generosity as socially required. Within such a perspective, therefore, tribute of this kind was sanctioned both by 'tradition' and by political practice. Those who selected the chiefs, as well as the mass of the rank and file, expected nothing less than the operation of such a rent mechanism. It was thus not just normal; it was socially desirable, even necessary.

Of course, such conception of chiefly status went hand in hand with a notion of chiefly responsibility, which was primarily *collective*. This is crucial since status could not be maintained unless chiefs discharged their duties and fulfilled their responsibilities. Although many of the attributes of the pre-eminent political leader were of a symbolic, judicial and religious nature, not a few of their functions related to the economic well-being of the community as a whole. Chiefs were due tribute but they in turn were expected to dispense benefits to those over whom they ruled. The nature of such obligations may not have been easily assessed in strict economic, let alone monetary, terms but it was nevertheless well understood locally by all those who belonged to the 'community'.

The wealth accumulated through rent was partly to be expended for symbolic purposes, as part of the periodic manifestation of political status and embodied power. Vast amounts of money could be spent on festivals, on the upkeep of religious shrines or on the organisation of burials. On occasions such as the passing of the chief, sacrifices might be required, of either cattle or even humans (usually slaves) – sacrifices that could seriously deplete chiefly capital. But it would be wrong to overstress these events, spectacular as they could be, or to deduce from their symbolic centrality that they were the main purposes to which wealth was devoted. More commonly, and more frequently, chiefs were expected to redistribute their wealth for economic, political or symbolic reasons.

The colonial period broke this link between power and obligation by forcing chiefs to work for, and account to, the imperial authorities. One of the consequences of this change in the nature of chiefly power – especially among appointed chiefs who viewed their position primarily as an opportunity – was that the office came over time to be seen instrumentally as a device for accumulating resources. Although there obviously were huge differences between chiefs during that period, as a rule the dissolution of accountability downwards to the population induced a shift from collective responsibility to a more individual quest for power and wealth. This transformation was facilitated, when not overtly encouraged, by the colonial authorities, who saw chiefs merely as auxiliaries and sought in effect to buy them out cheaply by making it clear they would sanction personal accumulation so long as political compliance was guaranteed. Since in most instances chiefs were entrusted with the responsibility of collecting taxes and, often, delivering labour, the scope for (legal and illegal) accumulation was vast.

The most significant colonial legacy in this respect was not that chiefs were suddenly able to enrich themselves personally, which they often were, but that they became (more or less) detached from the moral and social matrix within which they had hitherto related to their people. This not only resulted in growing inequalities within local society but it led to a break with 'tradition' in that power no longer went hand in hand with collective responsibility. Some chiefs might continue to behave honourably but the use (and abuse) of what the colonial authorities defined as customary law effectively gave the chiefs powers they had never had before. Conversely, it contributed to the disenfranchisement of ordinary people. Protected by colonial authority, the chiefs could afford to act far more 'irresponsibly' without fear of collective sanction. Clearly, they remained part of the locality and were still subject to religious and spiritual constraints but their political position no longer lay so firmly in the hands of those over whom they exercised authority.

In this respect, the consequence of colonial rule was the notion that power conferred possibilities of rent-making that were not sanctioned by collective responsibility and local accountability. More generally, it induced a mentality whereby all those who exercised some degree of power (e.g. interpreters) within the colonial administration felt entitled to negotiate it for personal benefit. This is, incidentally, one of the reasons why work in the colonial administration became so popular as a means of social and economic advancement. By the time of independence, therefore, the instrumental nature of the link between power and rent had become well established, both for the political elites and for the bureaucrats. Obviously, there were significant numbers of politicians and civil servants who were genuinely devoted to an ethos of public service and collective responsibility. But it is well to point out that there had occurred a dangerous breach between power and accountability, which had fateful political consequences after the end of colonial rule.

The final issue I would like to highlight is the impact of *aid transfers* on rent since independence. Given the socio-political and economic context of independence, it was natural that post-colonial politicians should have sought to claim foreign aid from the former colonial powers and, more generally, from the international community. There were good objective reasons why newly independent countries needed assistance after they became independent. There were also good geopolitical grounds – chief of which was the Cold War context – for the granting of aid from various Western and Eastern donors, which must also be taken into account. My interest here is not so much with the reasons for such aid but with the impact of these transfers on politics in Africa. Two points in particular need to be stressed. The first is that foreign aid eventually came to distort the post-colonial economy. The second is that it provided a massive boost to rent-seeking.

Foreign aid distorted the economy in four major ways. It placed African economies at the mercy of those donors who wanted primarily to further their economic interests in that country, regardless of its development priorities. It encouraged African governments to continue to put trade before industry in so far as the Western donors' main interests lay in the ongoing purchase of raw materials at the lowest price. It provided additional funding for the upkeep of a state bureaucracy and machinery that could not be sustained in the long run. Finally, it created a situation where African rulers became in some fundamental ways more accountable to outside donors than to their own people. This replicated what had happened to the chiefs during the colonial period.

However, where aid transfers were perhaps most damaging was that they made possible greater and greater rent-seeking among those who held power. Amplifying what had happened under colonial rule, the relationship between political elites and outside donors made possible an ever closer convergence between power and rent. Divorced from its moral and ethical base, power offered virtually unlimited opportunities for politicians, who could in this way accumulate vast resources without having to account directly to the population. Naturally, over time they came to realise that power without accountability took a toll on their legitimacy. Other than coercion, their only way out of this dilemma involved the reactivation of the 'traditional' politics of reciprocity and the economy of obligation, which had sanctioned status-linked rent in the pre-colonial period.

The outcome was a form of modern patrimonialism, often dubbed neo-patrimonialism, in which the equation between power and rent was not questioned so long as politicians agreed to redistribute some of their wealth to their clients. This apparent 'return to tradition' offered a possibility for both patrons and clients to make rent-seeking more acceptable. However, this meant that politicians became increasingly dependent on rent and that the object of power became more narrowly focused on rent-seeking, often at the exclusion of any other ambition. Paradoxically, then, the emergence of a form of modern patrimonialism consolidated even further the notion that power was about rent.

This has become a major problem today both economically and politically. Economically because there is less incentive for investment – that is, deferred consumption – which would inevitably reduce the amounts available for neo-patrimonial redistribution. Politically because it means that competition between politicians reinforces the nexus of power and clientelism at the expense of other forms of accountability, which would allow greater scope for longer-term policies favourable to more sustained economic development.

The emphasis in this chapter on striving serves to highlight the fact that ordinary Africans live in an economic world that is severely constrained. What we observe today is a situation in which historical, socio-cultural and political factors conspire to offer politicians excessive opportunities and to deny the populace the means to thrive. The advent of a near universal neo-patrimonial dispensation has been made possible by the emergence of a 'modern' variant of the economy of obligation and the politics of reciprocity largely divorced from 'traditional' accountability. This allows forms of clientelism that satisfy some of the patrons' constituents but works against the possibility of the type of economic development that would benefit all more equally. It also leads to a 're-traditionalisation' of the present political economy in ways that are unlikely to facilitate such development. It puts a premium on the politics of surviving.

SIX

The politics of surviving

In the previous chapter, I looked at some of the key aspects of African economies as they have evolved since the end of colonial rule. Here, I would like to turn my attention to the micro-picture of what individuals do daily to sustain, and if possible better, themselves and their families in such an environment. Therefore, I deliberately leave aside an examination of Africa's national economies – for example, mining and oil industries; large-scale agricultural exports; commercial agriculture; tourism – to focus attention on some of the activities in which most Africans engage in order to make a living or simply to survive. It is not that these macro-economic factors are unimportant – they are not – but simply that they have been covered adequately by the numerous studies, reports and books that analyse Africa's formal economies.

There are in addition two important reasons to give primacy to the ground-level economic realities of the continent. The first is that, with the exception of Botswana, the exploitation of minerals and raw materials has not brought about either sustained economic growth or an improvement in the well-being of the population, even less an amelioration of their future prospects. In most instances, it is the reverse: natural-resource wealth has served as a rent for the elites, inequalities have increased and poverty has worsened. The second is that the major economic changes that have resulted from outside 'expert' recommendations (chief of which is structural adjustment) have – with some limited exceptions (Ghana and Uganda for a time) – failed to achieve their aims. Whilst they have led to a decline in the provision of social and human services, which has penalised the poor most harshly, they have not spurred a form of market economy providing an avenue of individual advancement for the majority.

The causes of this state of affairs are complex and were discussed in *Africa Works*, which argued that the lack of economic development has primarily to do with domestic political reasons, even if the influence of the world economy has not been kind to Africa.[1] In the preceding chapters, I have touched on a number of issues that have a direct bearing on these factors and that explain why the working out of historical, social and cultural trends in post-colonial Africa have been detrimental to the type of economic growth found in other formerly colonial territories – such as Asia. If such are the reasons for Africa's lack of development, then we need to cast light on the other side of the coin: the underbelly of economies that cannot, or will not, provide reasonably for the population. This means we must study how ordinary people engage in economic activities to maintain life and a degree of self-respect.

In order to do so, we have to put aside (at least for the time being) the standard developmental approaches, which focus attention on the formal economy, formal economic actors, aggregate economic flows indicators and formal sociological groupings. We must instead think outside these academic analytical categories and enter the realm of the *informal* – in at least two ways. One is to make the effort to analyse the informal with the same acuity as the formal. The second is to think of the informal as an area of activity that is not strictly economic but made up of a number of socio-cultural and political facets which are vital to the understanding of what is

---

1. Chabal and Daloz, 1999: Part III.

actually happening. Only then is it possible to give value to factors that are otherwise neglected and to explain the rationality of what may appear 'irrational' in standard economic logic.

Rather than concentrate attention on the actual economic activities in which Africans engage to survive, I have chosen to focus on three key processes that are central to most of these activities: *informalisation, networking* and *migration*. The reason for proceeding in this way is that it is probably the best way of building up a general picture of what is relevant to most people whilst providing a methodology that enables comparison across countries. It is also to show that the only way in which Africans can exercise agency is to ignore the boundaries of the national state. Or, rather, to explain how boundaries are both obstacles and opportunities for those who are trying to make a living through migration or trade. The politics of survival cut across the confines of the nation-state to which Africans have belonged since independence. In the realm of the informal there is undoubtedly the deployment of pan-African strategies, which connect people through borders and over large areas. This, as we shall see, also extends well beyond the continent.

INFORMALISATION

What I am interested in here is the interconnection between the informalisation of politics, discussed in *Africa Works*, and the workings of the informal economy, as is now reasonably well analysed in the standard economic literature. To that end, I want first to explain a little better what I mean by informalisation. The bulk of the social science literature on Africa defines this merely in terms of what is not formal – that is, for the economy, what is not reflected in national accounts. In *Africa Works*, we extended this definition to the political, where we considered the informal to be the politics that lay outside the workings of the country's constitutional arrangements. These approaches are narrow and somewhat limiting. I want here to consider a process of informalisation that encompasses both the political and the economic and that illuminates the relationship between the two.[2]

It is probably most fruitful to approach the concept of informalisation from a more historical and dynamic perspective. Historical in that it should be put in the context of the ways in which politics and economics have intersected since the pre-colonial period. Dynamic in that it should be seen as a matter of initiative and innovation rather than, as it is in standard social science, solely as a last resort on the part of those who do not partake of the formal. Therefore, the notion of informalisation should no longer be taken as an indication of what is not working in Africa but rather as the conceptualisation of that which is effectively taking place – the norm rather than the exception. Indeed, those who are involved in these informal processes do not consider that they stand below a notional 'lumpen' social class in the sociological pecking order. They view themselves as exercising legitimate agency within the environment in which they live.

Furthermore, informalisation here is not synonymous with 'traditional' – meaning, as it does in standard social science, backward, a drag on modernity. Just as the dichotomy between 'modern' and 'traditional' does not make much sense in the context of post-colonial Africa, that between formal and informal is equally uninformative, when not downright misleading. What informalisation refers to is precisely the process whereby the 'modern' and 'traditional' interact in a dynamic of agency that seeks to overcome existing constraints to living a 'decent' life. It also means that it is not possible to understand what might constitute the 'modern' and the formal in Africa without paying proper attention to the 'traditional' and the informal, which are normally cast aside as residual categories in Africanist political analysis. What is required is the ability to explain how a hybrid life

---

2. My notion of informalisation is different from that of privatisation, with which it is sometimes confused. For different reasons, it is also conceptually different from criminalisation, with which it is also sometimes associated. There is nothing 'private' or 'criminal' about the informal.

that encompasses all these normative categories makes sense to people who are striving to survive in difficult circumstances.

Therefore, I would like to stress how agency is applied to the opportunities that arise from the combination of 'traditional' and 'modern' in a process that subverts and exploits the formal. At a first level, then, informalisation means the use of the ill- or non-functioning formal and 'modern' sector. Three aspects are especially important: *state*, *money* and *borders*. They act as the foil against, or through, which informalisation operates. They provide the 'modern' set-up that is exploited in order to generate resources that would not otherwise be available. What applies to these three areas is also true of others like elections, commerce, industry, and so on. Noteworthy in this respect is that all participate in informalisation; it is not the preserve of the disenfranchised from 'modernity'. In fact, if the keepers of 'modernity' and the agents of the formal were not also active participants, informalisation would not function as it does. Of course, the politics of informalisation may not be what Africa most needs in the long run, but that is another question.

The main issues with the *state* have to do with how the process of its informalisation has opened numerous avenues of economic opportunities. This has taken two main forms. The first is that the state has served as a source of resources, which those in control have diverted for their own patrimonial purposes. Politicians and bureaucrats have conspired to undermine the efficacy of the state by depriving it of the revenues to which it was entitled *and* by diverting the activities to which it should 'formally' have been devoting its energy. This has weakened the state and reduced its ability to function. In turn, such degradation has diminished further the scope of the state's activities and opened up larger and larger areas to informalisation. It has also consolidated the hold of neo-patrimonialism.

The second is that the 'devolution' of the state's activities to the informal sector has enabled large numbers, both within and outside officialdom, to find new or additional sources of revenues. On the one hand, functionaries have started charging for performing the services they are contractually required to provide: from the most banal, such as passing out forms to which the claimant is entitled, to the most drastic, like charging out extra for allowing the provision of a public utility (water, electricity, telephone, etc.). On the other hand, given the failure of the state bodies to offer the services they are supposed to provide, private entrepreneurs have stepped in to profit from the opportunities thus created. This ranges from the supply of drinkable water to the provision of education (from primary school to university). These private businesses may or may not be sanctioned officially but they are the direct result of the dilapidation of state services and the disappearing provision of public utilities.

The failure of the state to perform its basic functions and, in particular, to ensure the delivery of primary services opens up an infinite number of possibilities for the informal sector. But there is more: the state may not be able to do what it is mandated to do but it is still vigorous enough to keep a check on what is being done informally. So, the operation of the informal is only possible if it is sanctioned, unofficially of course, by the officials in supposed charge. Politicians and civil servants thus can, as it were, earn informal additional income for failing to carry out their duties: an exquisitely delicate situation that generates revenue for a number of individuals and organisations at the expense of the management of the common good. From the point of view of standard economic rationality, this makes no sense. From the perspective of those who are trying to survive a failing economy, it is eminently rational – even if in the process those who are already rich get richer.

My argument is not that the state is failing everywhere in Africa but that it is failing enough to make possible an informal political economy of this type, which itself contributes significantly to the further informalisation of the economy. Even in countries (like Uganda, Ghana, Mali, etc.) where the state has been much improved (admittedly starting from a very low base) in the last decade, there are clearly limits as to how much it is able durably to institutionalise or re-institutionalise. It seems as though the efficiency of the state is limited by an implicit compact between rulers and ruled that it is *also* to be used to informal ends. Thus, the state, in its informal guises, provides revenues for the many whilst at the same time undermining the possibility that it can achieve a degree of effective institutionalisation that would obviate the need for such informalisation. And the nature of the state has a direct bearing on the other two aspects of the process I should like to highlight: money and borders.

The question about *money* in Africa is a simple (economic) one: how expensive is it? On the face of it this is a plain enough issue, easily settled by a couple of variables: money supply and exchange rate. In truth, however, the situation is far more complex and, again, messier. There are essentially three kinds of currencies in sub-Saharan Africa today: fully convertible CFA francs tied to the French Central Bank and thus to the euro;[3] currencies from oil-exporting countries like the naira (Nigeria) or kwanza (Angola); and currencies from economically poor countries with limited export revenues. These differ greatly but all three are subject to a process of informalisation.

Taking the last case first, here the problem is a shortage of foreign exchange, which leads to state control and thus to the twin problems of overvalued money markets and a black market in foreign currency. In this instance, the situation is clear: the price of money is that of the informal (and illegal) market. Individuals effectively have to pay a premium, or tax, in order to get foreign exchange. That tax can in practice be negotiated informally, thus providing sources of revenues for those in charge of exchange control. For their part, registered businesses are forced to pay the exchequer a rent on the overvalued local currency, which means they have an incentive to find a less expensive informal settlement with the authorities. Clearly, then, there is much to be gained by those who control the state in maintaining an artificially high foreign exchange level, even if that goes against the economic health of the country. They value rent

---

3. The CFA franc is used in twelve (formerly part of colonial French West Africa and French Central Africa) French-speaking countries and in Guinea-Bissau and Equatorial Guinea. It has a fixed exchange rate of 1 euro = 655.957 CFA francs.

more than export. If, as is the case of Zimbabwe today, they find it impossible to acquire the foreign exchange needed to maintain the country's basic infrastructure, they can ration imports and start printing money – both of which hit the poorest hardest and are self-defeating in the end. The price of money becomes ever higher; the economy becomes ever more informalised.

In the case of oil-exporting countries, the value of the local currency fluctuates according to oil production and the standard monetary variables (including the supply of money). In Angola, for instance, the kwanza has now become a strong currency. Here, it is the control of the amount and value of foreign exchange that creates the possibility of the informalisation of the economy. In effect, there are two currencies in circulation: the national and the dollar (or euro). Profit is made by those who have access to both, which is possible only by sanction of the state. Trade licences are also managed by the state. Because oil is an export that is easily controlled by the ruling elites, the rent it provides can be allocated to those who run the informal economy. Other than the few who have access to foreign currency by other means, such as smuggling, the control of money reinforces political mastery and provides the rulers with a convenient means of patronage.

Finally, in CFA franc countries the situation is slightly, though not fundamentally, different. Since the value of the currency is tied to the euro and the money supply effectively supervised by the French banking authority, there is no leeway in those areas. The official price of money escapes direct state purview. However, there remains regulation over export and import licences. As these have to be approved by the authorities, there is still ample scope for negotiation and informalisation. Officially, individuals and businessmen may be able to acquire foreign currency at will but there is still an overall limit to the country's foreign exchange balance, which is controlled by banking authorities tied to France. Therefore, it is in the allocation of the permits that give access to the foreign currency needed for international trade that the informal comes into play, as it does in other countries. Additionally, there is an illegal market in CFA francs: it attracts a premium from those who live in countries whose national currency is not convertible.

What these three different cases show is that in contemporary Africa, as in other parts of the world, money has an informal cost, above and beyond its normal economic price as determined under standard conditions by the level of the interest rate and the money supply. And this price is set by political rather than economic factors, producing in this way rent for the rulers and (highly unequal) economic opportunities for those who have to resort to the informal economy in order to make a living. Here again, therefore, it is the very juxtaposition of the formal and informal, the legal and the illegal, which produces a premium that conspires to maintain a dynamic inimical to the type of financial institutionalisation which is required for stable investment.

The same is true in respect of *borders*, which act both as obstacle and opportunity. Here, too, the role of the state is pivotal. Borders, which are the physical markers of a country's sovereignty, are not officially open to negotiation. Indeed, however feeble African states have been, rulers have never (other than in historically very idiosyncratic instances like Eritrea and Somalia) been willing, or able, to tamper with the colonially inscribed frontiers they inherited at independence. The reasons are simple. To question the legitimacy of any border would be to open up a Pandora's box; it would quickly undermine the very legitimacy of virtually all colonial borders and would unleash economically damaging conflicts. More important still is the fact that borders are one of the key economic resources on the continent. However arbitrary they are and however limited the reach of the state is in border areas, the very existence of national frontiers is an invaluable asset for many.

The cost of negotiating borders, which is wholly a product of their presence, leads to the establishment of both formal and informal markets. The former is in the hands of the authorities, who can choose to tax the movement of goods and people as they see fit. Such tax is enforced, with varying degrees of zeal and efficiency, by the agents of the state, who draw an informal rent from their position. The informal market arises either as a result of the subversion of the law – where, for instance, import/export restrictions are violated – or simply because it is cheaper to bribe the (civilians or military) gatekeepers than to pay the official tax on trade. Whatever the details, the point here is to stress the ubiquitous process of informalisation that characterises the transit of goods and people through borders between African countries. This is one of the reasons why, although it has perennially been advocated, regional free-trade areas have never taken root on the continent.

NETWORKING

This process of informalisation is intimately linked to the prevalence of networking in Africa's political economy of obligation. I have already shown how networks are at the heart of the politics of belonging and partaking. In both instances, relations of proximity and reciprocity provide the foundations upon which rulers and ruled, elite and populace, relate to each other within and across communities. Equally, I have indicated how notions of ethics and morality are based on the honouring of relations of social exchange and on how these relations influence the nature and conduct of politics on the continent. Here, I focus more specifically on the economic dimensions of networking and in particular on the impact these have on informal trading, which is the central economic activity in Africa.

This question falls awkwardly between the concerns of political science, sociology, anthropology and economics; for this reason it is rarely discussed in its multi-faceted detail. My aim in this chapter is to understand the politics of surviving and because of this I draw freely from these different academic disciplines. But I want first to make a remark about Africanist political science. The main limitation of the way it approaches this question is the fact that it confines it to the realm of the informal, which it conceptualises as being separate and detached from the world of institutional politics. In that reading, the informal is a subversion of, and is antithetical to, the proper and desirable functioning of the state. What I have stressed so far is that the informal is part and parcel of the formal and that they are most profitably analysed simultaneously and in relation to each other. This is especially true of networking, which relies for its operation on the active interface between the two.

Of course, networking is to be found everywhere in the world; there is nothing geographically specific. Therefore, what I want to discuss here is how the nature of Africa's socio-cultural and political realities, as presented so far in the book, lends networking the singularly central place it has acquired in the continent's political economy. I am also interested in how it conditions the politics of surviving. I concentrate on three aspects of networking that are especially important: the *collective*, the *religious* and the *political*.

The communal, or *collective*, aspect is the crucial one. All such economic activity (of which the Chinese, Indian and Lebanese diasporas are also examples) rely on family, kin or clan to engage in trade. Since exchange is overwhelmingly the main source of income for most Africans, those individuals (of all social positions) who earn a living in this way necessarily depend on the 'traditional' bonds of obligation and reciprocity that stand in lieu of the more usual 'modern' contractual obligations. There are groupings in Africa (for example, the Dyulas), whose activities go far back into the pre-colonial period, that specialise in commerce and that have developed the social and economic links that facilitate such economic activity. They have an edge but are by no means on their own. In the first place, they too have to rely on other networks to operate; they must thus transcend the immediate politics of belonging. Second, they constantly need to revise and update – that is, modernise – the ways and byways of their commerce, given that national politicians across the continent are determined to extract as high a rent from them as possible.

Furthermore, the present weakness of African economies means that larger and larger numbers of people seek to use networking in order to make a living. New networks are consolidated; older ones disappear. Competition between networks is intense and it is those who have the most extensive and most reliable set of arrangements who are likely to prevail. Not only, therefore, do individuals try to activate the collective networks to which they belong, but they also attempt to create or invent new ones – which are 'modern' in their genesis but 'traditional' in their functioning. Or, rather, 'modern' networks are erected upon the 'traditional' bedrock of the economy of obligation discussed above. The interesting phenomenon, therefore, is that the reliance on networking results in the further 'traditionalisation' of the economy and the increasing informalisation of society. Hence, communal factors, far from disappearing, are in fact becoming both stronger and more prevalent in the continent's contemporary political economy.

Today, there are innumerable large-scale networks, operating throughout the world, that rely for their operation primarily on a communal infrastructure and well-organised but wholly informal trade and banking mechanisms. These are largely unwritten, but the spectacular development of the mobile phone and electronic communication has made possible an exponential increase in the use of the 'modern' equivalents of the 'traditional' drum. Techno-logical advance has worked to strengthen, rather than undermine, the collective basis of African networking, adding thereby another dimension to a process of informalisation that had long sustained trade. Modernisation, in other words, has been the ally of 'traditional' channels of exchange and reciprocity – which, again, should not surprise us since 'modernity' is in this respect nothing other than modernised 'traditions', in Africa as elsewhere.

Among those channels, *religious* networks have been central. There are several good reasons for this. In the first place, religion has never been confined by colonial borders and has in this way provided ready-made networks for those who wanted to communicate and trade beyond national frontiers. All manner of religions, ranging from Islam to Jehovah's Witnesses, have served as support infrastructure for the organisation and development of informal economic activities. It is not just that religious links make possible easy connections between groups in different regions or countries. It is also that the moral and ethical code of conduct implied and enforced by religious commitment has provided a solid platform for the generation of trust that is the single most important factor in any commercial activity.

Second, there are a number of 'traditional' trading fraternities – of which the Dyula in West Africa or the Yao in Eastern Africa are perhaps best known – that are sustained by devotion to Islam. As a world religion with a presence in most countries in West, East and (to some extent) Central Africa, as well as across the globe, Islam is well suited to commerce. Indeed, there is a very long history of trading among Muslims, particularly between North Africa, the Middle East and Africa. Not only does Islam provide a fairly rigorous legal framework within which to trade, but Arabic offers one of the few world languages upon which to construct more elaborate networks than those that are merely based on an oral culture. Documents and contracts make possible more extensive and more complicated commercial transactions, which empower those who know Arabic. Brotherhoods in West Africa, for instance, have built their wealth upon a long commercial tradition, which has dominated trade in the region for generations. Even if competition is now intensifying, Islam remains a strong asset for networking within Africa and between Africa and the outside world.

Today, other religious organisations – of which the Pentecostal are perhaps the most successful – have invested heavily in informal economic activities and trade. Here the strong sense of community generated among those who are often the rejects of both 'modern' and 'traditional' society, allied with an enthusiastic devotion to moneymaking, have propelled business forward. This 'new' religion, linked as it is to powerful churches in the United States and sister organisations in other parts of the world (ranging from South

America to Asia), is not only a powerful vehicle for networking. It is also a strong challenger to the African state since it is often built from the ground up outside the 'traditional' networks of reciprocity and patronage that have long controlled national economies on the continent. Indeed, they represent today one of the most potent tests for the neo-patrimonial order and it is not surprising that where politicians fail to tame them, they seek to join or co-opt them. Such is the mark of success.

This takes us to the *political* aspect of networking, which is at the core of Africa's present political economy. As we have seen already, networking is crucial to the neo-patrimonial political dispensation. No political reform – of which 'democratisation' is the latest and most insistent – has yet managed to change this relationship between politics and economics. I have discussed elsewhere how this has affected the nature and operation of the state in Africa.[4] I want here to look at this political arrangement from the viewpoint of the ordinary person in Africa. How does neo-patrimonialism fit in with the politics of survival? The key here is to examine carefully the ways in which the interaction of formal and informal affects the behaviour of those who have few options in life. This will help us to tease out the rationality of this type of political networking.

The informalisation of the state means in effect that it cannot institutionalise to a degree that would open effective channels for the transmission of public demands and would allow the operation of a bureaucracy capable of implementing public policy. This has two major consequences. The first is that the state has steadily been losing legitimacy since independence; this translates into widespread dissatisfaction with formal politics and a gradual disenchantment with the absence of public services. The second is that it puts a premium on other ways of pressurising politicians, of which the most successful remains that of networking. Because the rulers can scarcely enhance their standing by means of the achievement of

---

4. Chabal and Daloz, 1999: ch. 1.

public policy, they themselves are keen to increase their legitimacy through patrimonial means. As a result, both rulers and ruled have a vested interest in keeping alive, and if possible making thrive, those networks that can serve them best. Of course, the two sides have distinct aims. The politicians want networks to muster political support. The local population seeks the highest possible return on their patrimonial investment. But these combine to maintain the primacy of networking as the most effective way of reconciling political participation and economic benefit.

An indication of how deeply rooted such a system is can be gathered from the effect of 'democratic' politics since the transition to multiparty elections took place in the late 1980s and early 1990s. Whilst 'democratisation' has made possible major political changes – a free(er) press, greater freedom of expression and of political organisation, the growth of civil society organisations, and so on – it has not led to the expected economic gains. Far from freeing the market for economic actors to avail themselves of liberalisation, multiparty politics has led to an ever more intense exploitation of networking for economic purposes. Political competition between rival politicians has brought about increasingly frantic resort to patrimonial largesse as a way of securing votes. Ordinary people, for their part, have realised that their votes are now more valuable in that they can negotiate their ballot for economic benefits. Therefore, one of the (obviously unintended) consequences of 'democratisation' has been the increased 'marketisation' of politics along informal lines.

Whereas the one-party system favoured a more 'traditional' patrimonial organisation, multiparty elections have introduced greater competition between different types of networking – all of which turn on the negotiation of political support for economic advantage. Paradoxically, then, the upshot of 'democratisation' has been the reverse of that which was expected, illustrating thereby the limitations of an Africanist political analysis that has failed to consider how 'traditions' affect the exercise of power. 'Democratisation' of that ilk has not resulted in a form of liberalisation favourable to the advent of

Western-style liberal democracy. Instead, it is the Western democratic blueprint that has been adapted to African 'traditions', creating in the process a hybrid political dispensation that is essentially informal, and that strengthens further the centrality of networking. Although it is plain that this is not a system that can be sustained at the macro-level in the long run, since it leads to a constant depletion of national resources (only partially made up by foreign transfers), it is still rational for ordinary Africans to resort to networking as the most effective way of surviving.

MIGRATION

The politics of surviving, however, are not confined to the domestic arena. Much as Africans nowadays undoubtedly feel themselves to be the citizens of a particular country, they also function within an international, and even global setting. Indeed, the assumption that the existence of the nation-state marks the 'natural' boundaries of regular economic activities is wide of the mark. Africans have always moved in search of work, goods and land, and it is not the erection of colonial territorial borders, later solidified into national frontiers, that has stopped them doing so. As we have seen, borders ought to be seen as areas of opportunity rather than as barriers. In any event, they are functionally non-existent for those who know how to bypass, or neutralise, border controls. However, it is not just frontiers between contiguous countries that are porous; Africans today travel far and wide in pursuit of economic opportunities.

We need to put to rest a number of myths about African migration. One is that this is a new phenomenon: Africans have always moved across the continent and even beyond. In fact, Africa was populated and settled by the movement of groups that sought out land and resources west- and southward. Although the colonial authorities tried to control migration across borders, they were never able to manage it. Africans continued to move in search of better (or less bad) economic circumstances or to flee oppressive labour policies.

This continued after independence. A related myth is that Africans are sedentary. Above and beyond the fact that there are a large number of nomadic groupings, the reality of modern Africa is that people are prepared to move for economic reasons – even if, as we've seen, they remain deeply attached to their locality of origin. The last misperception is that Africans seek today primarily to migrate to the rich West or the Middle East. Whilst there is no denying the constant flow of people towards these destinations – which makes the news because of the desperate means they employ and because of the fear of economic migrants in Europe – the reality is that intra-African migration is far more important.

Since pre-colonial times migration has been one economic option for Africans and there has always been good economic logic for this. The question is, therefore, how does migration today fit in the politics of surviving? Three contemporary processes have been critical here. The first is that the *attitudes* towards migrants have changed both within and outside Africa. The second is that there are now far more extensive African *diasporas* throughout the world. The third is that the ready availability of modern *technology* has transformed the nature of migration. These three phenomena have had uneven and sometimes contradictory influence but they have contributed to new types of activities that show clearly how 'traditions' adapt to 'modernity' in order to further economic ends. I discuss them in turn.

Attitudes towards African migrants have changed drastically in the last two decades. Where once they were able easily to move to other African countries to work and live, they are now the butt of xenophobic policies almost everywhere. Even foreign communities established in their country of residence for generations find that their activities, assets and even persons are becoming less secure.[5] This situation, which is primarily the outcome of an aggressive economic nationalism in countries that have failed to develop, is having perverse consequences. Instead of assimilating those whose

---

5. As discussed in Chapter 2.

economic activities are often valuable, such policies force them underground and in this manner increase illegal economic trans-actions that lead to the further informalisation of the economy. It also reinforces informal networking since in order to survive foreigners who are harassed need to establish links with those who wield power.

Unfortunately, economic nationalism does not result in more sustainable economic dynamism. From the forced appropriation of foreign businesses in Zaire and the expulsion of Asians from Uganda under Idi Amin to the expropriation of white farmers in Zimbabwe, the pattern has been clear: the grabbing of economic assets is wasted from the point of view of production. It is like a grassfire: bright at first but short-lived. Since those who are expelled are frequently successful entrepreneurs and businessmen, their de-parture turns out to be a net economic loss for the country, as was amply demonstrated in these three countries. The process has been the same everywhere: intra-African migrants are often economically dynamic, for reasons having to do with the ethics and mentality of migration, and their removal is counterproductive. In the long run, the removal of migrants is not only illusory but goes against one of Africa's central 'traditions' – a tradition built upon trade and the movement of people.

Outside Africa, and in particular in Europe, anti-immigration policies have made it more difficult for Africans to move in search of better economic conditions. Since there is a virtually unlimited supply of would-be migrants on the continent and since the means to contain such migration are limited, the consequences of this policy have also been perverse. First and most importantly, it has driven emigration underground in two crucial ways. Migrants now waste resources (and sometimes die) in order to migrate, having recourse to unreliable go-betweens who claim to arrange for their move to the West. This feeds an important mafia-type economics that is of no benefit either to the migrants or to their country of origin. Yet more damaging, it pushes migrants to integrate into the informal *illegal* international economy, which is the only one that will make possible their migration. Whereas most of these migrants would have been prepared to work hard and legally in their country of destination, they now link up with powerful illicit networks that control the flow of illegal resources across the world, using Africa as a platform.

The net effect of this change of attitude towards African migration has been almost entirely negative. It has fuelled the informal and often illegal economy. It has buttressed the ever greater informalisation of Africa's political economy. Indeed, this form of economic activity has served the powerful well but it has been more detrimental to ordinary people. Rendered economically fragile by the increasing difficulty of exercising the option of migration, Africans have become more dependent on underground, informal and often criminal networks. Their desire for migration has increased as a result of the failure of their national economies but their ability to migrate has been reduced, raising thereby the cost of that survival option. This has been economically wasteful and has been detrimental to the development of the continent. Unfortunately, the precarious nature of everyday existence in Africa has made migration ever more desirable. It is now a vicious circle.

In one way, however, migration has become easier: there are now sizeable African diasporas in many more countries than there were even twenty years ago. If Africans have long been settled in the former colonial metropolis, they are now to be found almost everywhere. Today, even countries that had no historical link with Africa (Scandinavia or Eastern Europe) have sizeable African minorities and there are large groups settled in North America. Given the importance of (legal and illicit) trade flows between Africa and Asia, African businessmen and -women are now firmly established in countries like Malaysia and Thailand and even active in traditionally more closed areas like Singapore and Taiwan. Perhaps the most astonishing growth area has been in the United States where, it is alleged, Nigerians now control a great deal of the drug trade, at least on the Eastern Seaboard.[6] Equally, large numbers of Africans have settled in South Africa – provoking xenophobic reactions, and not just from the whites.

The point here is to stress how successful Africans have been in establishing themselves, even in countries where they had little presence and where they are not welcome. This is significant in two ways. It shows how Africans are able to migrate and settle everywhere despite the obstacles placed in their way, thus laying the foundations for the further growth of diasporas. Once there is a critical mass of Africans in a country, it becomes much easier to facilitate further migration, even if by illegal means. Clearly, Africans have been very adept at navigating the difficult waters of migration into the United States. Second, the emergence of these diasporas contributes to the growing international character of African identity. There are today large communities of Africans from particular countries, or even particular regions, who maintain active personal, family and financial links with their localities of origin, thus adding an increasingly important foreign dimension to the self-definition of those communities. One now speaks commonly of Dutch Ghanaians, New York Yorubas or American Ashantis.

But perhaps the two most important aspects of this pattern of settlement are that Africans living in Africa are increasingly dependent on the remittances from their compatriots abroad; and that this form of internationalisation reinforces, rather than weakens, the 'traditional' basis of the networking that sustains these migration flows. What this means is that the increasingly international character of the economy of the continent, much of it informal (and often illicit), is a powerful force for the maintenance of the present situation. Not only does it depend on the full deployment of the links of reciprocity and obligation that are the backbone of identity politics but it necessarily implies a connection with the world of local politics. Because these emigrants generate huge revenues for their

6. United States, Department of State, Bureau for International Narcotics and Law Enforcement Affairs, *International Narcotics Control Strategy Report*, Washington DC, April 1995.

kin back home and because they need to surmount, or bypass, the legal or illegal hurdles African states impose, emigrants (however rich and successful) must placate the local politicians. African rulers thus benefit in this way from an additional rent, which serves to extend their patrimonial reach.

Finally, members of the diasporas must also respect the local 'traditional' authorities. Because of the importance of the locality of origin both for identity and for networking, those economically successful members who live overseas must defer to the keepers of local culture *and* propitiate local authorities in the appropriate manner. This implies a form of communal participation that (as in the case of all emigrant communities) contributes both to buttress the existing socio-political order and very often to support a form of neo-conservatism – sometimes against those local members of the locality who would want to modernise 'traditions' more radically. This exerts an influence upon local politics, not all of which is of a kind that Africanist political scientists can explain or even understand.

The political and financial involvement of emigrants in their community of origin has been greatly facilitated by the ready availability of modern *technology*. The access to an ever expanding number of destinations easily reached by air has made it possible for Africans to move freely and quickly between countries and continents. Even if intra-African air links are still patchy, they are now much better than they were twenty years ago. On the other hand, connections between Africa and the rest of the world are booming, not just as in the past through Europe but now more and more frequently through South Africa, the Gulf, South and Southeast Asia and even the United States. Prices, though still high, are coming down with increased competition. The decision of Virgin Atlantic to fly to Nairobi or Lagos is emblematic in this respect and Emirates now fly to more and more (commercially active) African destinations.

However, it is perhaps the mobile phone and the Internet that have most revolutionised the nature of migration and the role of African diasporas. The availability of mobile networks has placed cities, towns and most large villages in Africa within range of telephone communication. Almost all Africans now have access to telephone connections with the rest of the world, even if only a minority are able actually to pay for the phone calls. This is an astonishing development, which has brought diasporas into immediate and continuous contact with their locality of origin. Today, business is conducted almost entirely by means of mobile-phone technology. The ability to work in real time has added a whole new dimension to the other trading skills Africans have always possessed. They can now compete on level terms with others – for instance by access-ing information about market prices for a number of commodities. Finally, the rapidly increasing access to the Internet – there are now cybercafés in all African cities and towns – provides the possibility of fast and reliable written communication, which is of course invaluable for diaspora economic activities.

Modern technology has transformed the place of migration in Africa. Where before, emigrants left (usually for good) to make a life elsewhere and came back episodically whilst sending remittances as and when possible, they now remain much more closely connected, and involved, in local community affairs. One indication of the im-portance of this change is the fact that witchcraft has now also moved into the modern technological age. Witches are routinely believed to move across continents, usually at night, and thus to affect com-munities both in Africa and abroad. In other words, 'tradition' has fully incorporated technological progress and has in this way ensured that diasporas remain an integral part of the local community – in every possible aspect, including the occult. This is proof, if proof were needed, that the modernisation of Africa is unlikely to follow the course Western social theories have set in stone.

This discussion of the politics of surviving has stressed the im-portance of the 'traditional' bonds of reciprocity and obligation that make possible financially rewarding economic activities. It has shown how individual agency transits through collective channels of belonging and how the strength of social relations serves the cause of economic achievement. Yet again, there is evidence of the resilience and flexibility of the networks, which protect and support those who are engaged in the search for economic success. At the same time, this chapter has shown that such strategies of survival result in what might be called the 're-traditionalisation' of socio-cultural, economic and political activities in contemporary Africa. Not only do these practices rely on the use of 'traditional' networking but they also provide the resources that feed a continuous process of informalisation. Paradoxically, therefore, the politics of surviving makes it more difficult to achieve the reforms that would contribute to greater political institutionalisation and more promising economic development prospects in Africa.

SEVEN

The politics of suffering

As the previous two chapters have demonstrated, Africans are both resilient and ingenious in the management of their straitened circumstances. Many succeed, even if they do so in ways that are not obvious or that remain invisible to the uninitiated observer. Unfortunately, this is not the whole story. If the ability to survive is not in doubt, neither is the depth of suffering endured by the millions of desperately poor people who have no access to the clientelistic networks that are so essential to life in Africa.

It has often been remarked that in the last ten years, and from a general perspective, GDP is growing healthily on the continent. Yet a closer analysis shows that this is primarily due to the revenues of mineral or oil exports – and is not the outcome of internal economic growth sustained by diversification and the export of transformed or industrial products. In other words, economic growth is largely driven by the revenues from primary product exports and by foreign aid. And the revenues so generated either 'disappear' (for instance in oil-producing countries) or are shared on a limited and patronage-linked basis. As a result, poverty is increasing for the majority of the population, and rises in GDP go hand in hand with greater inequality. The upshot is the continued increase in the number of poor people.

Africans also suffer because of the dereliction of the state. It is not just that most governments have failed to implement development policies that would bring benefit to a large proportion of the population. It is also that rulers have used the state for patrimonial purposes, so in the process eroding its capacity to carry out its basic functions. The gradual weakening of state institutions, and especially of those social, health and educational provisions on which ordinary people depend, has affected most deeply those who have no patrons and no means of buying these services privately. Furthermore, the almost universal degradation of public infrastructure (roads, transport, water, electricity, communication, etc.) has, again, affected the poorest and most deprived disproportionately. The same is true of inflation, of course, since the fall in the value of local money affects unduly those who have no access to convertible currency.

The informalisation of the state also brings further trouble for the powerless in that it increases everyday arbitrariness. Indeed, the less the state functions as it is supposed to do, the more it becomes a source of exploitation. Not only do ordinary people meet constant demands for kickbacks in their daily dealings with state officials but they are also subject to the whims of all of those who can exercise some degree of power over them. Civil servants, therefore, prey on those who cannot afford to resist them: police harass ordinary people; nurses demand bribes; teachers require payment; the providers of official paperwork (ID cards, passports, market licences, etc.) sell their 'good offices'. In the absence of effective sanction, these abuses are widespread and completely random from the point of view of their victims. What works today may not work tomorrow. Officialdom becomes an obstacle course, to be avoided at all costs. This, it is plain to see, fuels further the recourse to informal protection, if it can be afforded. The point here is not just that abuse is constant but that it is arbitrary; it can never be properly anticipated or guarded against.

I have touched on all of these issues, even if implicitly, in the previous chapters. I want here to focus more specifically on what have become the three most acute forms of suffering on the continent: *violence, conflict* and *illness*. I recognise that the everyday impediments to normal life and, more generally, the absence of economic development are probably the most perennial and immediate sources of despair for the bulk of Africans. However, I would like to explore in greater detail what is most likely to take them over the edge. Whatever the quibbles over numbers, it is clear that vast numbers of Africans are dying from violence and illness. It is thus not possible for any student of Africa, let alone any Africanist political scientist, to avoid thinking analytically about these issues. Sadly, these are not mere calamities visited upon the land by the wrath of God. They are largely political and man-made catastrophes.

If some analysts argue that violence is decreasing in Africa (which is debatable), no-one believes that illness (of which HIV/AIDS is only the worst) will cease to affect ordinary Africans in the near future. Indeed, even where HIV/AIDS appears to have peaked, there is still an increase in death from preventable diseases, such as malaria, dysentery and those other afflictions that arise from malnutrition, the absence of clean water or proper sanitation. As students of ill-health know, the greatest cause of disease is poverty. So long as poverty grows, so will disease. One final remark: however harsh some of the following analysis may appear in its conclusions, it is as nothing compared to the suffering endured by most Africans most of the time. Africanist social scientists cannot avert their eyes because some of the conclusions they reach may turn out to be unpalatable to political elites.

VIOLENCE

I make a distinction in this chapter between violence and conflict for two reasons. One is that I want to explore forms of violence that do not result in conflict. The other is that I want to examine conflicts not primarily through the prism of the violence they inflict, awful as that may be. Indeed, what is terrible in Africa is not just the degree of overt and physical brutality, which can be very high, but the huge range of violence visited upon ordinary people on a regular, if arbitrary, basis. At its most extreme, it might be the use of starvation as a political weapon or the forcible displacement of people to regions of a country that are unsuited to agriculture, where they sink into poverty, despair and hunger. Or it can take the form of the social and psychological trauma endured by young people who are compelled to commit crimes (e.g. mutilation, killing) on their kin. Equally, it can transit through witchcraft or religious sanctions, which again fall heavily on children and which provoke severe psychological damage. I am not arguing here that any of these terrible forms of violence are specific to Africa. I am merely saying that they have all happened in the recent past and, if not simultaneously, often in rapid sequence – with frightening results.

Even more insidious in my view is what might be called the calculated violence of neglect; that is, the deliberate failure of governments and state officials to carry out their duties in order to benefit from the ensuing disorder and distress. Again, this may not be true in all African countries. Nor am I unaware that some officials themselves suffer grievously from their own terrible circumstances. I am only pointing out that ordinary men and women are often the pawns of politicians in whose interest it is to exploit, or benefit from, poverty and ill health. Numerous as are the professionals who are truly devoted to public service – among whom are the bulk of the health profession – in most countries this is not sufficient to ensure the most minimal delivery of reasonable services. There are many who accomplish miracles every day but they, too, are faced with officials who simply do not care. Dedicated individuals and even functioning organisations cannot operate with any degree of effectiveness over time in an environment of infrastructural and governmental dilapidation.

Violence of that nature is significant because it has long-term institutional and personal effects. I will return to the institutional consequences below. Here I want to concentrate on the personal ones. The overall consequence of a state of such generalised violence is a process of dehumanisation. This takes at least three forms: the *degradation of the human body*, the *collapse of shared values* and the *breakdown of social order*. Of course, these occur wherever violence is endemic. However, what is worrying in the case of Africa is the fact that the abuse visited upon ordinary people has been so persistent and insidious. Conflicts can be brutal but they stop. Violence of the type I describe is like a low-grade fever that never ends. Although Africans have shown how resilient they are, it is probable that such persistent subjection to an arbitrary and continuous form of brutality is having long-term psychological effects we do not yet fully understand. This is why I think it is crucial to think more systematically about these three aspects of everyday abuse.

In the first place, then, this process of dehumanisation affects the person by way of the *body*. The prevalence of living and working conditions that are not suitable, most particularly in the city, results in a life of malnutrition and of unsanitary conditions. Generation after generation of people are born, live and work in circumstances that are simply not acceptable. The effects are multiple, ranging from chronic illness (as I discuss below) to stunted physical or mental development. Children living in such environments are confronted with enormous, usually insurmountable, odds in their quest for a better life. Leaving aside their social handicaps, their very physical person is already at a disadvantage, making them more prone to disease and less able to go to school or work. Since Africa is urbanising at a dizzyingly rapid pace and since conditions in the cities are not likely to improve, or improve fast enough, the prospects for generation upon generation of young people is unremittingly bleak.

These conditions produce an environment in which bodies are relentlessly degraded. The violent conditions of life are made worse from the constant risk of actual physical harm that can be suffered at any moment at the hands of the police, rival gangs, thugs or militias. Because people are often beaten up for no good reason, there develops a culture of overt brutality that comes to permeate more and more thoroughly the everyday way of life. Parents are abusive; children behave violently to other children. These conditions, which are produced throughout the world by hunger, poverty and lack of opportunities (as in Rio de Janeiro's *favelas*), are made very much worse in Africa because violence is pervasive everywhere in society, and not just in the shanty towns. There are now whole regions, sometimes countries, in which there has been a state of acute generalised violence for years, if not decades. Children are born in areas where complete disregard for the body, and the person, are simply routine if perhaps not yet 'normal'.

Although the well-known cases of Mozambique, Sierra Leone, Liberia, Rwanda, Uganda and Somalia usually make the headlines, the more worrying aspect of the present situation is the ever greater development of a culture of political violence. In many countries (e.g. Congo, DRC, Nigeria, even Kenya) there are now myriad youth militias – some set up by politicians; others self-generated – that are now organised like alternative 'societies'. Young people, generally cast adrift by social and economic circumstances, are hired or organise themselves as political gangs, community self-defence forces or just simply criminal bands. Detached from their roots, they inhabit a world of brutality within which there is little respect for the body, or the person. Drugged or not, they think nothing of inflicting the most harrowing physical pain, torture or mutilation. They kill as a matter of course. There arises in this way a culture of brutality that dehumanises those who use as much those who suffer violence.

The constant violation of the body is both cause and effect of the *collapse of shared values*. Youth militias are only able to function as they do because they are no longer bound by the values attached to their communities of origin. That much is clear. However, it would be misleading to view them merely like urban gangs in the West, for instance. Their detachment from society is both more complete and more worrying, for reasons having to do with the nature and role of communal norms in contemporary Africa. Although youth brutality is only one symptom of current violence, it is especially ominous both because young people are now the majority on the continent and because their break with societal norms is likely to have widespread, long-term, consequences. The present situation in Kinshasa, for example, where hordes of young people roam the streets, both victims and perpetrators of violence, is perhaps an extreme case but it is illustrative of a social disease that is gradually permeating society with insidious force. Young boys and girls are, for example, routinely accused of witchcraft and brutally punished, when not killed outright.

The effect of the collapse of shared values, which everywhere provide the glue binding society together, is profound. Violence undermines the norms and beliefs that sustain the place of the individual within the community. It hacks away at the sense of belonging, which is intimately connected to the notion of identity that lies at the heart of the socio-political networks of obligation and reciprocity. When these values no longer manage to keep the community from strife and destruction, they lose purchase. At first it may only be a section of the community, some youth, who no longer fit and therefore cease to belong. In the end, however, the break between generations can have fatal consequences for the group. When young people are cast out, they reject the prevailing ethos, cease paying respect to their elders and discard authority. Since they no longer 'believe', they can no longer be sanctioned. Deprived of cultural and moral foundations, they cease to belong. They thus lose their identity and seek solace in a form of 'nihilism' that can easily lead to self-destruction and that in any event cannot ultimately be countered by force.

Protracted poverty, migration, urbanisation are all made worse by a culture of violence that reduces the worth of the individual and destroys the communal foundations of their existence. This demeaning of values contributes greatly to dehumanisation because it is not the result of the slow, 'natural', process of value change. It is a brutal and arbitrary rupture from what had hitherto formed the backbone of people's moral and social world. It is not that they have ceased to believe in the norms that governed their lives; it is that they are forced into circumstances that make it impossible to live by those beliefs. Even youth militias, who are convinced that they are the masters of their own fate, are in fact the victims of endemic violence. Because values are collapsing around them, they are socially disenfranchised. No longer part of the circle of life to which their generation belongs, they are open to abuse and exploitation. Communal norms and beliefs have betrayed them. Now effectively dehumanised, they seek identity and respect in violence.

The generational rupture is one of the many symptoms of the *breakdown of social order* − by which I mean not merely the fraying of 'traditional' values, which might be seen as a sign of 'modernisation', but rather a state of generalised moral, cultural and socio-political anomie. I am concerned with the effect of this state of affairs upon the relationship between norms and behaviour. I have argued that what are labelled 'traditional' beliefs and values continue to provide the ethical framework of political action in contemporary Africa, even if politics is officially conducted according to the rules of 'modern' liberal democracy. If that is true, then the nature of the intertwining of the 'modern' and 'traditional' is of especial importance to social order. Or, to put it another way, the ways in which 'traditions' modernise is critical − as of course it has been everywhere else in the world.

A process of modernisation that involves too radical a fracture with 'tradition', as do revolutions, is only achieved by force. Where violence is directed purposefully to certain political ends, it can contribute to the construction of a new society − even if that society collapses later, as did Communist Russia and Eastern Europe, because 'modernity' was imposed against 'traditions' that continue to resist. Where, however, such rupture is the result of arbitrary and directionless violence, as is most often the case in Africa, it carries the greater danger of offering nothing meaningful or substantial as a substitute for the 'old' values. The apparent breakdown of the 'traditional' social order is not just of anthropological interest; it is of immediate consequence for the type of society found today on the continent. It has two contradictory effects, which combine to undermine the coherence of the social order.

On the one hand, there are numerous disenfranchised groups (chiefly youth), many of which will never be reclaimed by any meaningful or viable social order. They are likely to drift through life seeking economic and political opportunities by means of violence. For them, violence becomes the vain quest for a 'human' identity. This is very disruptive of society, even if politicians blithely assume they can exploit such youthful anomie to their own personal ends. On the other hand, the failure of 'modernity' to provide the moral framework within which change can be managed adequately leads to the continuing 're-traditionalisation' of society. This means not that people are returning to traditions but that they seek in 'traditions' the means by which to make sense and manage their everyday lives. In so far as violence permeates society, this process needs to provide an antidote. As is well illustrated by the role of witchcraft in contemporary Africa, that antidote itself can also be predicated on violence.

The impact of violence on African societies, therefore, is both penetrating and long-lasting. It degrades individuals, dissolves social norms and deflects human energies from more productive activity. It also corrodes the process whereby 'traditions' are modernised and in this way contributes to the weakening of the social, ethical and cultural foundations upon which Africans can exercise agency. It is a poison that is damaging to the prospects of development. The way out of this infernal circle is not obvious, especially given the prevalence of conflict. However, to acknowledge the nature and depth of violence in Africa is not to say that the continent is doomed. There are today many initiatives to break out of this cycle, and the consolidation of electoral political systems can provide one way of putting pressure on politicians. Africans are weary of violence. The question is how to avoid perpetuating it.

CONFLICT

Conflicts inflict violence in ways that are well documented. The record of wars and conflicts in Africa since the 1960s is, by any standard, appalling. Whatever the number of victims, Africa has clearly suffered a surfeit of armed clashes, ranging from local strife to civil or inter-country wars involving thousands of combatants. Some, notably within Angola and between Ethiopia and Eritrea, have seen conventional battles that compare with the worst anywhere else. Other civil wars, as in Sudan or the DRC, are protracted and consist of episodic violence aimed chiefly at forcing people to move away from areas of dispute. Most of the time, however, conflict is lower grade: outbreaks of armed hostility between regional groups; militia attacks on economic targets or on civilians; warlord armies indulging in (often vicious) guerrilla tactics; and bouts of army involvement in local or cross-border fighting.

Directly or indirectly, conflicts in Africa have affected millions of people in almost all parts of the continent. Indeed, it has become easier to list those countries where no conflict has taken place (e.g. Botswana, Cape Verde) than the reverse. What has made conflict in Africa so damaging, however, is that it most often targets civilians deliberately. Even when armies fight each other openly, they resort to force against civilians as an overt instrument of war, thus magnifying suffering immeasurably. This has happened elsewhere in the world, of course, but not on the same scale and not so systematically. Indeed, recent conflicts in Africa, with the exception of the Ethiopian–Eritrean war, have largely been directed against civilians. In other words, the warmongers attack, brutalise and kill civilians as a way of achieving their aim, not as a by-product of their armed action. War against civilians has become the norm, not the exception.

Conflict, therefore, is not an episodic calamity but an endemic condition, which affects a large proportion of the continent's population. Above and beyond the effects of violence I have discussed above, I would like here to look at the debate about the causes of conflict and about their possible resolution. In order to do so, I want to move away from the normative position that consists in decrying conflict per se, as if it were merely a form of illness that needs eradicating. Appealing as this approach might appear to be, it is simply too ahistorical. Human societies have always suffered violence so that the question is not whether conflicts can be abolished but what they mean in their local context and what their long-term consequences are likely to be. The interpretative tension here is between those who favour *cultural, structural* or *economic* explanations. Let me review them before offering my own conclusions.

Cultural explanations, which have a long history in Western Africanist work, hinge on a simplistic causal model. In the first place, it assumes that Africans are divided along tribal, ethnic or other similar ascriptive lines – deemed to be the dominant, if not sole, markers of identity. Second, it posits that the juxtaposition of such differences in identity leads inexorably to conflict. Evidence for this viewpoint is adduced from pre-colonial history, which is often seen as a period when inter-group violence was supposed to be widespread. Although it is true that in the decades that preceded the imposition of formal colonial rule there was considerable violence in some areas of southern and central Africa, this had identifiable historical causes and had nothing to do with an inherently hostile 'state of nature', as it were. The justification that the imperial nations had to conquer Africa to put an end to violence is nothing but *ex post facto* rationalisation, and in any event colonialism was itself a regime of considerable (overt and covert) violence.

Today, the cultural explanation reappears constantly in different guises.[1] It is still the most common account of the violence in Rwanda and Burundi, and it is deployed in respect of conflicts as far apart as the DRC, Sudan and Sierra Leone. The Western press continues to portray Africa as a land of 'ancient tribal hatreds' as though this

---

1. Of which the most insidious is perhaps that illustrated by Robert Kaplan's thesis on Africa's 'new barbarism', only somewhat tempered by his later book. See Kaplan, 1994, 1997.

could serve as a catch-all explanation and as though similar ethnic conflicts were not found elsewhere, including in 'modern' Europe. Cultural explanations, therefore, are not plausible even though they refer to aspects of conflict in Africa that are undoubtedly real and relevant. The fallacy in the argument rests in its essentialism. There is a conflation of two processes, which results in a pseudo-explanation. The first is that much of this violence exhibits markedly 'traditional' features. The second is that there are a large number of conflicts between different identifiable social or ethnic groupings. So let us unpack this sleight of hand.

If there is deadly conflict between the Hutus and Tutsis in Rwanda and Burundi, it is not because they are, respectively, Hutu and Tutsi, endowed with an unambiguous identity and a 'traditional' hatred of the other. It is because the historical circumstances of their living and working together since the nineteenth century were irredeemably altered by colonial rule, setting one against the other, and because economic constraints (chiefly land shortage) created a fiercely competitive situation. Since independence, politicians have played the card of political tribalism, mobilising support and hatred along ethnic lines. It is their systematic and unrestrained exploita-tion of this difference, to which all others were made subservient, that created a situation in which political rivalry engendered ethnic conflict and, eventually, degenerated into genocide.

Here, as almost everywhere else in Africa, the causality is the reverse of that suggested by the culturalist explanation: it is political manipulation of 'difference' in a context of socio-economic hardship that triggers ethnic conflict. That such violence should be channelled along 'traditional' lines is nothing more than should be expected, in Africa as in the rest of the world. Indeed, current communal violence in our own societies is similarly linked to ethnicity. However, there is no evidence that 'traditional' markers of identity are the *causes* of violence; they are merely its most convenient channels.

Structural explanations of conflict point to the weaknesses of social and political institutions in African countries. Here there are two different types of interpretation. On the one hand, there are those (the majority among Africanist political scientists) who argue that such institutions are not *yet* strong enough to maintain order and contain violence but that they will develop in due course. On the other hand, there are those who contend that existing Western institutions are not *adapted* to African conditions and that conflict will not be muzzled until effective 'African' structures are in place. Although the gap between the two is important – indeed, there seems to be no halfway house – these two dominant approaches share certain assumptions. They both presume that conflict and violence can only be reined in by adequate institutions. Furthermore, they both presume that there are identifiable causes of conflict – which causes can be addressed by structural means.

Both of these have merit and are certainly relevant to an overall explanation of the prevalence of conflict in contemporary Africa. There is little doubt that the lack of institutionalisation in, and in many cases the de-institutionalisation of, Africa has contributed greatly to the state's inability to prevent, contain or resolve conflict. And it would be no exaggeration to say that the continued weakening of the state will make it increasingly difficult to reduce violence on the continent. However, structural explanations are limited because they fail properly to ascertain the extent to which the 'modern' structures of the state have been 'traditionalised' in the ways described in earlier chapters. If, to resume a previous argument, the formal is at the service of the informal, then it is impossible to conceive of a type of institutionalisation that would not be undermined by this form of overlapping.

My point here is that the standard social-science approach to the question of conflict simply omits to give equal consideration to the two sides of the coin, the formal and informal. They either ignore the issue or assume that once structures are properly institutionalised the informal will somehow wither away. Those who favour a more African approach, on the other hand, find it difficult to explain how indigenous institutions would reduce conflict. How, for instance, does one integrate ethnicity into a political dispensation that gives fair representation to the different groups without leading to an ever more severe competition between them for state resources? The problem here is not that conflict is *caused* by the informal but rather that it travels along myriad informal and 'traditional' channels, which shape its complexion and affect the ways it impinges on ordinary people. Structural explanations thus need to account for the informal.

Economic explanations are perhaps the most common. They range from the ubiquitous argument that poverty fuels violence to the notion that 'greed' prompts people to use conflict as a means of acquiring more resources. This is a debate that goes well beyond Africa but I will focus on what is directly relevant to the continent. The thrust of this line of argument is that a lack of economic progress or the prospect of economic opportunities is the primary cause of violence. This is a powerful argument, which stems from a strong common-sense conviction that deprivation fuels resentment and resentment results in conflict. Broadly true as this may appear to be, it is in fact a very poor predictor of either the occurrence or the resolution of conflict.

The flaw in the assumption that deprivation is the main cause of conflict in Africa is not so much that economic factors are irrelevant, which plainly they are not, but that there are so many other variables. A causality of that type is a simplification of the question that borders on frivolity. The greed-versus-grievance hypothesis has added a degree of complexity but it has centred attention on a pseudo-dichotomy that is neither very helpful analytically nor a very realistic rendering of a reality far more complex.[2] Economic factors are important but how they translate into violence is essentially a result of historical, social and cultural factors that can only be properly assessed in their local context.

Indeed, the relevance of any explanation of conflict is more likely to lie in the fine grain of the contextual detail than in the generalised

2. Collier and Hoeffler, 2001.

proposition. There is simply no single economic cause of conflict; economic factors play themselves out through a number of contingent and contextual circumstances. For instance, historians of revolutions know that the key economic factor in sustaining violent action is not absolute but relative deprivation – which is another way of saying that those willing to support a revolution must have some notion of what a better, but achievable, economic condition would be – even if they turn out to have deluded themselves. As concerns current conflicts in Africa, the most recent and most sophisticated conflict alarm systems pay greater attention to a host of factors, including a combination of political, socio-economic and strategic elements.[3] Conflict is often a deliberate policy choice.

ILLNESS

Violence and conflict have also had a dramatic impact on illness, the prevalence and effect of which have grown in recent years. If Africa has long been seen as the land of disease – a view that derives from the Europeans' inability to survive on the continent before the modern medical age – the colonial period undoubtedly saw vast improvements in hygiene, health and medical care. Both the development of tropical medicine and the implantation of a modern medical infrastructure contributed greatly to a decrease in mortality, better living conditions and a substantial growth in population. Indeed, the situation at independence was relatively promising: most countries had a reasonable health-care system in place as well as a good number of trained health workers, including specialist doctors. However, the gradual deterioration of the post-colonial state has led to a rapid decline in both health standards and the provision of medical care. With few exceptions, health conditions have worsened considerably in the last two decades.

3. African Union, 2002; Brecke, 2000.

This situation was aggravated dramatically with the outbreak of HIV/AIDS in the 1980s, the spread of which has now become a pandemic in all African countries, save for some in West and North Africa.[4] Today, both the UN Human Development Index and the figures for life expectancy illustrate the collapse in health and the widespread increase in illness that currently affect Africa. In point of fact, it is not just that mortality has risen drastically; it is also that even those who are not afflicted by HIV/AIDS have a considerably worse quality of life than they might have had twenty-five years ago. A number of preventable diseases – such as malaria, river blindness, cholera, and so on – are now on the rise again, a sure sign that basic health care and treatment have declined considerably in the recent past. In most countries, health provisions are simply inadequate, when not non-existent, and people are left to resort to what 'private' or 'traditional' medicine has to offer. Those who can (including the political, business and bureaucratic elites), go abroad for medical treatment; the rest suffer ever more.

My interest here is less in offering a survey of health and disease in Africa than it is to think through their socio-political implications within an overall discussion of the increase in suffering on the continent. Whilst it is sometimes argued that illness is the cause of poverty and wretchedness in Africa, it is in a fact a symptom of its general social, economic and political condition. Despite the devastating impact of the HIV/AIDS pandemic, it is clear that the prevalence of disease and ill health is the result of the precarious situation in which most people live and work on the continent. Africans are not poor because they are ill; they are ill because they are poor. The question of health, therefore, must be set within the overall context of the political evolution of post-colonial Africa.

The study of illness is revealing in this respect because it focuses attention on the main political issues that matter the world over: governance, accountability, policymaking and implementation, public

---

4. Iliffe, 2006.

service, efficacy and human development. It is customary among Africanist political scientists to attribute the shortcomings in health provisions to a lack of resources and training. It is equally customary among African politicians to argue that these shortcomings are the result of punitive structural adjustment programmes, which have crippled governments and forced a reduction in social expenditures. Both are right in no small measure but both fail to look at the bigger picture within which the decline of health has taken place. The delivery of adequate health provisions is not a mystery. It consists of three parts: the country's general infrastructure, the training and proper employment of health professionals, and the allocation of sufficient resources. All other issues, important as they may be (for instance, whether to privilege preventative medicine or to decentralise health care) are subsidiary to these three key aspects of the question.

Clearly, it is not to be denied that illness has economic consequences, which are usually highlighted by experts and the media: the incidence of HIV/AIDS deprives Africa of so many able-bodied people and reduces potential GDP growth by so many percentage points. However, this is an approach that obscures more than it reveals, since the reasons for ill health and poverty are basically the same. Furthermore, it prevents understanding of why, even with massive transfers of resources to Africa designed to ameliorate health and combat illness, the general situation is scarcely improving – even if the impact on the treatment of AIDS has been noticeable. Therefore, I propose to tackle this issue differently by looking at the political implications of the health situation in Africa from, respectively, *social*, *psychological* and *religious* viewpoints. This is not meant as a substitute for the more usual study of illness and health from the medical, sociological or economic perspective but merely as a complement to what is already addressed in the literature. As will become immediately apparent, these three aspects are closely inter-related.

Illness in Africa is a *social*, and not an individual, phenomenon in several important ways, which have a bearing both on how it is experienced and on what effects it has on people and communities.

This is true throughout what might be called the cycle of illness. The acknowledgement and perception of ill health are deeply rooted in a collective sense of identity in so far as it is seen as a reflection of possible social factors, linked to questions of identity and belonging, which are believed to affect well-being. A disease is not a mere 'accident' and, consequently, it affects all those who are part of the social network concerned, regardless of the nature and origins of the ailment. Parents, relatives and kin are concerned by the affliction and feel themselves implicated in its diagnosis and treatment. The decision as to whether to go for 'traditional' or 'Western' medicine is likely to be a collective one.

It is in this area that the decline in health provisions has had the most profound impact. Since today modern medical care, where it is available, is not free, the question of money is crucial. Although the fees are often modest, the cost of treatment and medicine is relatively high, if not prohibitive, for most people. Access to it, therefore, is almost always dependent on the pooling of collective resources for the benefit of the individual who needs treatment. Family and kin are the first line of defence but there are also in Africa innumerable 'traditional' and 'modern' solidarity networks, which rely on regular payments by their members and provide a form of social security. At a most practical level, then, the ability to face illness is eminently social. Without solidarity of this sort, ordinary Africans simply cannot afford access to health care.

Finally, the treatment of illness is social in yet other ways. When a hospital stay is necessary, it is only possible if the patient is supported and looked after by relatives. Hospitals in Africa require that family feed, clean, provide bedding and look after the patient. In addition, medicine must usually be purchased, often outside the hospital, which means that a crucial part of treatment also hinges on the social network. Similarly, if the patient is unable to work, it is often the relatives who take over his/her activities, so that occupational income does not come to a halt just when the family has greater needs. Finally, any convalescence is the responsibility of the network since there is little provision for post-hospital care in the community. Therefore, without an adequate social network, Africans cannot avail themselves of medical treatment or medicine; nor can they get the resources to subsist whilst unwell.

Given the social nature of illness in Africa, its *psychological* impact is different from what it is in the West, and different in ways that matter for the understanding of everyday life. Typically, illness and accident are believed to have identifiable causes, which need to be exposed before they can be addressed. I will discuss below the religious aspect of this phenomenon; I want here to focus on what impact this has on behaviour. The tension between 'traditional' and 'modern' explanations of ailing is one that has always lain at the heart of the approach to illness in Africa. Falling ill has an immediate psychological impact, above and beyond the physical affliction, since it imputes causality somewhere, often among relatives or kin, who may wish one ill. It is a sign of weakness, or rather of the susceptibility to being affected by outside influences, which can result in ostracism or rejection. People who are ill are psychologically vulnerable to outside pressure and influence.

The retreat of modern health care has limited the possibility that people can in fact receive Western medical treatment, since it is now more difficult than ever to find the money to pay for 'modern' health provisions. As a result, patients must again rely on 'traditional' medicine, which involves a large degree of psychological diagnosis and treatment, some of which is quite onerous. The effects of the regained primacy of 'African' medicine (which, of course, had always maintained an important place even when Western health care was more readily available) is to restore a sense of the importance of the 'traditional' in the conception of what ill health actually entails. In this way, therefore, it also contributes to the further strengthening of the process of social 're-traditionalisation' I have already discussed at some length.

From a psychological point of view, therefore, illness in contemporary Africa goes against the process of individualisation, which sociologists have asserted as necessary to individual 'modernity' and which some social scientists have argued is taking place on the continent. The point here is not to argue, simplistically, that there is a reverse process of de-individualisation taking place. It is to suggest that the current process of individualisation is unlikely to run along the smooth single-track lines so cherished of Western social scientists. It is much more likely to continue to embody the collective 'traditions' of obligation and reciprocity, which have always had an influence on people's sense of identity and their notion of their place in the social order. It is also likely to impinge on the way they conceive of the machinations of politicians. After all, the elites can always buy good treatment; indeed, far fewer now die of AIDS, which is fast becoming the disease of the poor.

The social and psychological aspects of illness are part of the more general *religious* context within which ailment is understood and addressed. Since untoward events such as accident and disease need to have an explanation, their cause is likely to be cast in terms of the existing belief system. This is true everywhere, as the yearly spectacle at Lourdes, or Fátima, reminds us. So the point is to try to assess how local beliefs affect the approach to ill health. Here, the deliquescence of modern medicine has been widely interpreted as the failure of Western 'science' to cope with current afflictions in Africa. Therefore, it has reinforced the place of 'traditional' systems of rationality, which at least do offer explanations for afflictions and propose treatment to cure illnesses. As the failure of 'traditional' medicine actually to cure people is itself built into the existing belief system, there is little to challenge its explanatory power when modern medicine is not available. The failure of treatment must have another cause!

In such circumstances, it is not surprising that witchcraft should continue to occupy a central place in the acknowledgement, diagnosis and treatment of ailments – even those, like HIV/AIDS, which most people already know to be most successfully treated by Western medicine. It is short-sighted for analysts to consider witchcraft as a separate sphere of belief; it is in fact at the core of the local religious world-view. Its existence is not at issue; what is at stake is the influence it has on people's well-being. Where, as in some Western American fundamentalist religious communities, HIV/AIDS is seen as God's punishment, there is still no hesitation in resorting to modern medicine for treatment. However, the situation in Africa is different: the belief in a socio-cultural or religious cause of illness leads to the application of 'traditional' medicine — with disastrous consequences in the case of illnesses like HIV/AIDS.

My point here is not to use the emotive issue of HIV/AIDS to cast a stone at 'tradition' but simply to stress that the notion of illness and the approach to its treatment in Africa must be firmly set within the religious matrix within which people live, and die. The current situation in Africa in which modern medical care is limited, when not derelict, does not just impact on people's health. It also contributes strongly to the belief that 'modernity' has little to offer ordinary people, even in the one area, health, in which colonial achievements seemed to have been so objectively spectacular. The failure of the state to deliver reasonable health care is one of the strongest factors in the loss of confidence that its 'modernity' can provide what people need. Whether, as social scientists tend to believe, 'modernity' would in due course reduce the hold of 'traditional' beliefs in Africa is a moot point, since in respect of health it is found wanting. And since the elites, too, partake of the beliefs that continue to give witchcraft a hold on people's lives, why should ordinary people believe any differently?

Africans show great resilience and infinite ingenuity in their struggle to live a decent life. And they do 'smile' a lot, as Fela Kuti used to sing. In recent years, however, they have also suffered grievously from violence, conflict and illness — the combination of which have had disastrous effects. Here I have attempted to show that the consequences of these three disorders are politically profound. They undermine the belief in the effectiveness of the state; they contribute to the breakdown of social order; and they boost a process of 're-traditionalisation' that is not favourable to development. Ultimately, they set back the cause of a type of 'modernisation' that would contribute to the improvement of people's lives.

Conclusion

At the end of this journey into the politics of everyday life in the postcolony, what have we learnt about Africa? I indicated at the outset that I was less concerned with theory than with *insight* and that theories ought to be assessed on pragmatic rather than conceptual grounds. Therefore, this book is not primarily an argument for or against particular theories but rather a study in the politics of Africa, understood broadly, which aims to offer as sharp an understanding of local realities as can be mustered. However, there is in the book an underlying theoretical framework, a form of theorising, I should like now to discuss more explicitly.

I do not conceive of theory in the abstract, as a model of causality to be applied to particular settings, because I do not believe social science should try to emulate the 'hard' sciences in this respect. Yet, most Africanist political science *is* predicated on such a model. The upshot is that we are used to reading political analysis as the application of specific theories to circumscribed areas of political life in Africa: governance, elections, democracy, state, civil society, political economy, law, international relations, and so on. If this can sometimes be useful as a comparative device, it is also constraining, if not downright misleading, for reasons I have tried to explain throughout the book.

Thus, the book has shown that it is fruitful to analyse what is taking place in Africa without recourse to a given political theory. I have pointed to many instances where standard Africanist political science obscures our understanding. My approach, which involves tackling questions that arise from what is actually happening on the ground, has prompted me to call upon various disciplines and various theories as and when needed. Hence, I have not tried to reconcile different frameworks into what I would call an artificial theoretical homogeneity.

However, I do not subscribe to the empirical dogma that only facts speak, as though facts stand out there, merely to be discovered; as though the way facts are identified, presented and connected does not matter. On the contrary, my reading of the evidence betrays a theoretical proclivity but one that does not start from the scientific pretensions of social science. Instead, as I have explained, it is based on a cultural approach that draws from what is called the interpretation of meaning, first mooted in anthropology by Clifford Geertz.[1]

What this method entails is simple to state, if more difficult to apply in practice. It is the systematic attempt to comprehend and convey what makes sense to people at the local level without prior ideological or theoretical agenda. This decoding, this interpretation of local meanings, requires translation into a language that enables comparative analysis – that is, a self-reflective presentation of the evidence as we, the observers, perceive it. In other words, it is not a claim to possess a privileged status, or vantage point, making for omniscient and objective appreciation of free-floating facts. Rather, it is an attempt to explain how we choose our evidence, why we interpret it the way we do, and how our choices matter for explanation.

---

1. I have written at length about this method elsewhere, so will only mention here the most relevant elements. See Chabal and Daloz, 2006.

The usefulness of this approach is twofold. On the one hand, it forces us to explain why and how we study what we do. We can no longer hide behind the theoretical screen of our discipline, which ostensibly commands the manner in which we ask the questions we are supposed to ask. This is a bracing exercise. Once they cease using standard variants of the comparative model of politics, Africanist political scientists have to start explaining why they privilege one approach over another. And in doing so, they must expose their work to theoretical scrutiny.

On the other hand, it enables us to consider questions we would not have addressed otherwise. This is beneficial since, relieved from the constraints of a disciplinary road map, we are free to navigate where the evidence takes us. We are, of course, influenced in this respect by our own vision, training, experience and prejudice. But since we stand outside the comforting theoretical surroundings of our discipline, we need to argue our case and convince our readers, which is more arduous if ultimately more rewarding. At the very least, it makes it easier to measure up and contest our interpretation.

I will say no more about theorising because, by the time they reach this conclusion, readers will already have been able to decide for themselves what insights the book may have provided about post-colonial politics in Africa. I want instead to close with a reconsideration of three key questions of comparative analysis, which lie at the heart of all Africanist scholarship. These are also questions that are critical to the debate about how Western social science approaches the study of non-Western parts of the world.

THE UNIVERSAL AND THE LOCAL

From the point of view of theory, the tension between the universal and the local is double. First, what should the *vantage point* of analysis be? Second, what *concepts* should be used? These are questions confronting the study of any society but they are particularly acute with respect to Africa because Africanist scholarship is constantly pulled in contradictory directions. Both sides of the Africanist debate move easily from universal to local agendas, depending on the issue.

Some point to the local determinants of particular processes (e.g. corruption, conflict). Others respond by identifying the global culprits (e.g. structural adjustment, multinational cupidity). Similarly, some argue that Africa should follow the universal path of development staked out in the West – it must go for capitalism and liberal democracy. Others claim that the continent is evolving in ways that are not best explained by Western theories, and analysts should employ concepts rooted in African realities.

The consequence of this confusion has been twofold. On the one hand, it has resulted in a dialogue of the deaf – by which I mean that students of Africa have spoken *at* each other from incompatible analytical perspectives. On the other, it has generated a giant theoretical potpourri – a mixture of approaches that have little in common. This would not matter overly if it were not for the fact that theories do have practical consequences. Given the complexity of the situation in Africa, policymakers are in need of 'expert' advice: what Africanists tell them, therefore, has serious implications. World Bank policies, for instance, are the product of the conclusions reached by its analysts, who themselves are influenced by outside debates.

What, then, should the *vantage point* of analysis be? There is a clash of at least three different rationales here. The first is the 'scholarly': the perspective of academic disciplines, in which standard Western comparative politics dominates. The second is the 'ideological': the perspective of those who allocate responsibility for the condition of Africa, of which the anti-imperialists (now anti-globalisation) have the edge. The last is that of 'authority': the perspective of those who argue that Western intellectual traditions hamper understanding of Africa, of which the post-colonial scholars are the leading group. This multiplicity of standpoints, which are not always openly declared, creates a state of theoretical confusion.

In the first place, therefore, it is useful to understand that the search for consensus is illusory. The best that can be hoped for in the review of the existing literature is to identify the perspective from which the various analysts work. Second, it means that little progress can be made in the political analysis of Africa until scholars are prepared to make explicit, and especially argue, their standpoints – that is, until they stop avoiding the real debates or indulging in theoretical broadswords.

Many Africanist political scientists, wanting to avoid controversy, tackle political interpretation from the safety of universal theories of development. Running large-N surveys, which mirror those carried out in other parts of the world, they explain Africa by dint of using methodologies applied everywhere else. For their part, a good number of African scholars dismiss comparative political science as the handmaiden of Western prejudices and resort to either post-colonial or political economy theories to explain the African predicament. Devoted to an attack on Western theories, they often neglect to address issues of immediate concern, such as state collapse or local violence.

This leads naturally to the question of what *concepts* should be used in Africanist political theory. Here, too, there is a strong tension between the universal and the local. This is a battle on two fronts. On the one hand, there is debate about whether concepts used in Western social science are able adequately to reflect African realities. On the other hand, there is the question of whether the selection of concepts does not overdetermine the type of evidence sought out and uncovered. This is an old problem, which goes back to the origins of anthropology and which has not abated since. What matters for our purposes is that we should be aware of the tension and that we should make clear why we choose particular concepts and how that is relevant for interpretation.

The weakness of Africanist political science in this respect is that it fails to discuss – or even to acknowledge there is a need for discussion of – the limitations of concepts drawn from Western (comparative) political theory. This is because it assumes concepts are universal. However, given that political science cannot be 'scientific' in the ways that its practitioners imagine, there can be no undisputed universal concepts. All concepts are historically and contextually generated and, therefore, bounded by the historical circumstances in which they appear. Paradoxically, therefore, they are in this sense local and not universal.

There is equally little justification for the (admittedly rarer) position that African realities are too complex to be explained by means of concepts other than *sui generis*. The old (but not irrelevant) debate about Négritude illustrates the problem. Senghor's interpretation was that Africa's modernity was not best captured by Western perspectives. Although his concern was mostly with the arts, the concept he coined gave the impression that there was an African 'essence', which was emotional rather than rational. Senghor actually put forward a far more sophisticated view of African culture than is usually acknowledged. But there is no denying that the manufacture of a local notion like Négritude obscured his interpretation – and made him vulnerable to Soyinka's later quip: 'does the tiger need to proclaim its "tigritude"?'

Here, I have attempted to address the tension between local and universal by offering a multi-pronged analysis. I have employed concepts that were in harmony with the local nature of the question *and* of sufficiently general purchase to be applied elsewhere. I have in this way tried to make the local understandable to those who wish to situate the politics of Africa within a more general comparative framework. The argument of the book in this respect is that it is simply impossible to privilege either local or universal at the expense of the other. What matters is the ways in which the two are married in the exposition of the material. An approach in terms of the interpretation of meaning works from the ground up but it is geared to translating the local into an account that is intelligible in the infinitely variegated language of human politics.

THE QUESTION OF GENERALISATION

In the Introduction, I touched on the issue of whether it was appropriate to write a book that generalised about the whole of the African continent. I pointed out that there was indeed a strong argument against generalisation, which needed to be taken seriously. However, I took the view that to invalidate generalisation on the grounds of diversity was to refuse to compare. I conceded that not all generalisations were appropriate or even helpful and argued that the value of a generalisation was not best gauged in the abstract but in the study of how much sense it made locally.

I now want to revisit this question more systematically and, as I close the book, review the value of the generalisations I have made in the chapters above. In standard political theory there is very little debate about generalisation: political science is built on the theorisation of what are taken to be general processes. The theory itself is a conceptualisation of such generalisations. The defence of political science against the charge that it applies irrelevant theories to Africa is that its generalisations are not Africa-specific; they apply to all modern polities, regardless of history. In this way, political theory guards itself against the allegation of ethnocentrism.

My position is more difficult since I have argued that Africanist political science was deficient precisely *because* it was universalising the application of its theory to the continent. If such is the case, then, I have to tackle the Africa-specific arguments against generalisation. Leaving aside the standard critique of generalisation, discussed in the Introduction, these can be bundled into two different categories. The first brings together the objections having to do with the projection of Western prejudice upon a reality that is not understood. The second argues that generalisations about Africa are constructed upon assumptions of Western 'superiority' that vitiate analysis. I take them in turn.

The first objection links up to an old debate, going as far back as Conrad's *Heart of Darkness*. Over a century later, opinions are as divided as ever and, interestingly, the arguments have not changed much. Those who attack Conrad – of whom Chinua Achebe is perhaps the most distinguished – claim that the Polish writer displayed all the racist arrogance characteristic of the European mind. To them, generalisation is always deployed to highlight the negative image of Africa. Their argument is that it is simply unwarranted to paint Africa with a single brush – a form of simplification, they argue, the West does not apply to itself. For instance, what happened in Bosnia is not interpreted as being 'representative' of Europe.

This is a powerful argument, which cannot ultimately be refuted on its own terms, since it points to racism. In response, I will limit myself to three observations. The first is that Conrad is often misread. The endlessly quoted 'savagery' and 'abomination' at the end of the book refer to the Romans' first impression of Britain – pointing to a general and not Africa-specific condition. The second is that it is incumbent upon social scientists to explain what they witness, however unpalatable that explanation. The last is that it is not the analyst who creates the realities of poverty, violence and illness found in Africa today. To deny the validity of an interpretation merely because it is derived from a generalisation is to deny the very essence of research-based analysis.

The second set of objections is ultimately more lethal, since it strikes at the very heart of social science. And there is indeed merit in the charge that Western social science is predicated on the theorisation of Western supremacy. Does this mean that it cannot generalise about non-Western areas on the grounds that it cannot transcend the forms of conceptualisation that are the foundations of Western social science? It is a question I shall tackle in another book.[2] My explanation of the type of generalisation made in this book is fourfold.

First, it does not derive from a theoretical *a priori*. On the contrary, it stems from a critical stance vis-à-vis a type of political science that

---

2. Provisionally entitled *Western Rationality after Post-Colonialism*.

applies all too unreflectively the conceptualisation of Westernisation to non-Western areas. My starting point is that we must be wary of making assumptions about the nature and sequence of development processes as they are built into existing political theories of Africa. Since it is impossible to be devoid of assumptions, the only useful option is to make them plain.

Second, my approach – the interpretation of meaning – is designed to prioritise the research task of trying to make sense of local circumstances. What this entails is the resort to a very large range of evidence stemming from the whole gamut of the social sciences and humanities and a willingness to consider the theories under-lying these different disciplinary research activities. This necessarily induces a critical stance in respect of the assumptions and certainties displayed by social science.

Third, I favour a comparative rather than Africa-centred type of explanation; I am more interested in uncovering what is common to human behaviour than what is singular. I have tried to get answers to what might be called 'generic' questions within an African context. Generalisation of that type helps us to make sense of people's lives in terms understandable outside the local context.

Final, and crucially, there are in contemporary Africa a large number of common political processes, which invite comparison. Indeed, it is the blatant similarities between countries, regions and peoples that appear at first to be quite distinct, which have forced attention on the need for generalisation. The general has emerged from the local evidence, brought to light by a large number of scholars (both African and Western) working on entirely different material. That cannot be coincidental.

THE PITFALL OF ESSENTIALISM

Yet, even if the case for generalisation is accepted, there remains the charge of essentialism – by far the most damning indictment. The defect of essentialism is easy to explain if somewhat more difficult to establish. In a nutshell, it involves a two-step type of reductionism. The first is to claim that given groups of people are endowed with a certain set of attributes, which can be identified and classified. The second is to deduce from these alleged attributes types of mentality, beliefs, thinking or behaviour, which are supposed to 'explain' why these groups act as they do. This type of explanation is tautological, or circular, since it amounts to selecting characteristics that will in turn be taken to cause some course of action. Moreover, it cannot be challenged since it asserts what it then employs as a means of explanation.

Before we reject, as we must, essentialist explanations, it is well to consider that in most instances they are drawn from clichés, which are plausible enough to acquire commonsensical authority. Indeed, this type of essentialism is found everywhere. Thus, it is sometimes claimed that the Germans are disciplined, the French argumentative, the British upright, the Italians devious, the Arabs dishonest, the Chinese inscrutable, and so on, *because* they are German, French, British, Italian, Arabic and Chinese. As I move on to discuss Africa, I want to make two remarks. The first is that, because clichés are ubiquitous, they deserve attention. They are but a frivolous way of expressing our vision of the 'other', which reveals as much about us as it does about those we stereotype. The second is that clichés ought to be taken seriously by social scientists for the simple reason that they reflect 'popular wisdom', which forms part of the world in which we live.

The problem about an essentialist explanation is dual. First, it is very largely a self-fulfilling account of 'others' since, once in currency, it is generally impervious to new evidence. It is thus a form of self-dialogue that has little to do with a genuine desire to understand the 'other'. Second, essentialist characterisations are built upon relations of power between groups. As we know only too well, clichés demean those considered to be inferior. The issue about essentialism is not so much the need to rule it out of court on normative grounds, which is simple and straightforward enough, but to understand how it operates in our own thinking. This is much more difficult because it appears to be a 'natural' enough way of telling ourselves why 'others' are as they are. A categorical rejection of essentialism, though self-satisfying, leaves out the more intricate, and more necessary, analysis of how it may acquire respectable social scientific status.

I discussed in the Introduction the reasons why the study of Africa by non-Africans is, quite rightly, sensitive. Given the history of the colonial 'encounter' between the West and Africa, it is especially difficult for Western scholars to escape charges of imperial scholarship. This is as it should be. The assumptions of Western scholars should always be challenged most vigorously. As a final contribution to this debate, then, I conclude with a personal reflection on (1) what it means to avoid essentialism and (2) how to offer one's work to critical assessment. I discuss in turn two key objections to Africanist scholarship: *oversimplification* and *ethnocentrism*.

Oversimplification is probably the most often cited weakness of Africanist scholarship. This is a perfectly valid, and very often correct, critique of our work. Indeed, much social science, and by no means only on Africa, is guilty of this felony. Let us try to unpack what this means concretely. The charge covers two separate issues, which need to be addressed separately. The first is that *social science* itself tends to simplify beyond what is good for analytical purposes. This has to do with method rather than intent. The second is that social scientists oversimplify what they write about *Africa* because they believe that realities on the continent are simpler than they are in, say, their own societies.

I have sympathy for the first critique: social science does indeed oversimplify. It is for this reason that I've offered a methodology that does not draw on Africanist political theory as it has been practised in the last few decades. An approach in terms of the interpretation of meaning may be difficult to achieve but it cannot be charged with oversimplification. Of course, my analysis is open to challenge but at least it lays down clearly the method from which it is derived. The challengers will need to give more plausible accounts.

The second critique also has merit although I believe it has been overused. It is disingenuous to claim that social scientists wilfully consider Africa to be 'simpler' to understand than other settings. It would be more accurate to say that some of them tend to oversimplification, regardless of research area. But others do not. In the end, we are back where we started: namely, whether there is something in the Western gaze upon Africa that induces oversimplification. This is not an issue that will be settled by abstract discussions. It will be for each one of us to tackle it as best we can.

I now move to *ethnocentrism*, which is also a logical way of closing the book. My starting point is that it is more useful to recast this issue in terms of the more general problem of standpoint. This makes it possible to move away from the emotive implication that such defect is linked to some form of 'racism'. And it focuses attention on the more fundamental difficulty involved in any comparative research enterprise.

In this respect, I think it is useful to distinguish two aspects of the question. One has to do with the conceptual difficulty of taking into account the subjective nature of the analyst's standpoint. The other is to build into the analysis the relations of power between researcher and 'subject'. Both of these challenge social science as it is practised today. At the same time, however, neither is specific to Africanist scholarship; this is a general conundrum, which stands in the way of all comparative work.

What makes ethnocentrism such a sticky issue is that it strikes at the heart of social science, for the problem of reference point has no simple answer. The assumption made by standard political science − namely, that a scientific approach in terms of theory, hypotheses, data gathering, and so on − is itself sufficient guarantee of analytical objectivity is questionable. Unlike the 'hard' sciences, where it is possible to operate on the basis of such axiomatic and epistemological presumptions, not to mention the broad agreement of what a 'fact' is, the social sciences cannot escape the ultimate dilemma of subjectivity.

For this reason, I think it is preferable to acknowledge this 'existential' problem from the start rather than obscure the issue by claims of scientific neutrality. Social scientists need to be explicit about their point of reference. This involves two steps: one is to be self-reflective at every stage of the research and interpretation; the other is to seek to make one's work more, rather than less, contestable. However, to do so requires method and it is in the specific application of the method that the problem is best addressed.

Among the important issues that need tackling is a full justification for the research involved. It is not enough to say that a particular topic is a legitimate object of study for social science. It is critical to explain why it merits attention now – which might include subjective reasons, personal experience or current affairs. It is also imperative to justify explicitly the methodology used. Again, it is not enough to assume that the deployment of standard social science methods is unproblematic. Method and the purpose of the research are linked in a reciprocal analytical relation that needs explaining.

In the end, however, this will not be enough. It is impossible to avoid the issue of the relations of power between researcher and research subject. This is a general difficulty which afflicts all social science research and this relationship cannot be other than problematic. In the case of Africa the problem is compounded for historical as well as contemporary reasons. The one is the outcome of the history of colonial conquest, which has locked Europeans and Africans in a long and bitter relation of exploitation. The other derives from the fact that post-colonial Africa has failed to develop, for reasons that are contested and impinge on the way in which research is conducted.

The attempt in this book to discuss political theories of Africa has involved a double helix, as it were. On the one hand, I have tried to show why much current Africanist political science is deficient.

On the other hand, I have expended my efforts in applying a mode of analysis that aims to provide a more ground-level account of how politics is played out locally. Clearly, this has meant that I have left aside many of the common topics covered in the Africanist literature. This is partly because there is little need to go over the same ground again. But it is largely because I remain convinced that what is needed now is a new approach to the same questions: to cast a different light on contemporary Africa that will provide insights rather than certainties. Advance in the social sciences does not mean progress. There is no unilinear development in the acquisition of a greater 'truth', merely unsteady steps towards more enlightening knowledge. As one of Africa's greatest writers put it more simply, 'Les choses qui ne peuvent pas être dites ne méritent pas de noms.'[3]

---

3. 'What cannot be said does not deserve a name.' Kourouma, 1970: 151.

Bibliography

Abélès, M., and H.-P. Jendy (eds). 1997. *Anthropologie du politique*. Paris: Armand Colin.

Abrahamsen, R. 2000. *Disciplining Democracy: Development Discourse and Good Governance in Africa*. London: Zed Books.

Abu-Rabi', I. 2004. *Contemporary Arab Thought: Studies In Post-1967 Arab Intellectual History*. London: Pluto Press.

Achebe, C. 1975. *Morning Yet on Creation Day*. London: Heinemann.

Adibe, J. (ed.). 2008. *Who is an African? Identity, Citizenship and the Making of the Africa-Nation*. Lagos: Adonis & Abbey.

African Union, Assembly, First Ordinary Session. 2002. *Protocol Relating to the Establishment of the Peace and Security Council of the African Union*. www.africa-union. org/root/au/organs/psc/Protocol_peace%20and%20security.pdf.

Aho, J. 1999. *This Thing of Darkness: A Sociology of the Enemy*. Seattle: University of Washington Press.

Ake, C. 1979. *Social Science as Impeialism*. Ibadan: Ibadan University Press.

Akindés, F. 1996. *Les mirages de la démocratie en Afrique subsaharienne francophone*. Dakar: Codesria.

Allen, C. 1999. 'Warfare, Endemic Violence and State Collapse in Africa', *Review of African Political Economy* 81, pp. 367–84.

Almond, G. 1990. *A Discipline Divided: Schools and Sects in Political Science*. Newbury Park CA: Sage.

Almond, G. 1996. 'Political Science: The History of the Discipline', in R. Goodin and H. Klingeman (eds), *A New Handbook of Political Science*. Oxford: Oxford University Press.

Almond, G., and G. Bingham Powell. 1966. *Comparative Politics: A Developmental Approach*. Boston MA: Little, Brown.

Almond, G., and J. Coleman (eds). 1960. *The Politics of Developing Areas*. Princeton: Princeton University Press.

Almond, G., and S. Verba. 1963. *The Civic Culture: Political Attitudes and Democracy in Five Countries*. Princeton: Princeton University Press.

Almond, G., and S. Verba (eds). 1980. *The Civic Culture Revisited*. Boston MA: Little, Brown.

Amin, S. 1972. 'Underdevelopment and Dependence in Black Africa', *Journal of Modern African Studies* 10(4).

Amselle, J.-L. 1990. *Logiques métisses: anthropologie de l'identité en Afrique et ailleurs*. Paris: Payot.

Amuta, C. 1990. *The Theory of African Literature*. London: Zed Books.

Anderson, B. 1983. *Imagined Communities*. London: New Left Books.

Anderson, D., and V. Broch-Due. (eds). 1999. *The Poor Are Not Us: Poverty and Pastoralism*. Oxford: James Currey.

Anderson, D., and R. Rathbone (eds). 2000. *Africa's Urban Past*. Oxford: James Currey.

Andreski, S. 1968. *The African Predicament*. London: Michael Joseph.

Anyang' Nyong'o, P. (ed.). 1987. *Popular Struggles for Democracy in Africa*. London: Zed Books.

Appadurai, A. 1996. *Modernity at Large: Cultural Dimensions of Globalization*. Minneapolis: University of Minnesota Press.

Appiah, A. 1992. *In My Father's House: Africa in the Philosophy of Culture*. New York: Oxford University Press.

Apter, A. 1992. *Black Critics and Kings: The Hermeneutics of Power in Yoruba Society*. Chicago: Chicago University Press.

Apter, D. 1955. *The Gold Coast in Transition*. Princeton: Princeton University Press.

Apter, D. 1961. *The Political Kingdom in Uganda*. Princeton: Princeton University Press.

Apter, D. 1965. *The Politics of Modernization*. New Haven: Yale University Press.

Apter, D. 1973. *Political Change: Collected Essays*. London: Cass.

Armah, Ayi Kwei. 1968. *The Beautyful Ones Are Not Yet Born*. London: Heinemann.

Ashforth, A. 2000. *Madumo: A Man Bewitched*. Chicago: University of Chicago Press.

Augé, M. 1982. *The Anthropological Circle: Symbol, Function, History*. Cambridge: Cambridge University Press.

Augé, M. 1983. *Le sens des autres*. Paris: Fayard.

Austen, R. 1987. *African Economic History*. London: James Currey.

Ayittey, G. 2002. *Africa Betrayed*. New York: St Martin's Press.

Babu, A. R. 1981. *African Socialism or Socialist Africa?* London: Zed Books.

Badie, B. 1986. *Les deux États: pouvoir et société en Occident et en terre d'Islam*. Paris: Fayard.

Badie, B. 1992. *L'Etat importé: l'occidentalisation de l'ordre politique*. Paris: Fayard.

Badie, B., and P. Birnbaum. 1983. *The Sociology of the State*. Chicago: Chicago University Press.

Bailey, F.G. 1969. *Stratagems and Spoils: A Social Anthropology of Politics.* Oxford: Blackwell.

Balandier, G. 1957. *Afrique ambiguë.* Paris: Plon.

Balandier, G. 1967. *Anthropologie politique.* Paris: PUF.

Balandier, G. 1971. *Sens et puissance: les dynamiques sociales.* Paris: PUF.

Balandier, G. 1980. *Le pouvoir sur scènes.* Paris: Balland.

Balibar, E., and I. Wallerstein. 1991. *Race, Nation, Class: Ambiguous Identities.* London: Verso.

Banton, M. 1997. *Ethnic and Racial Consciousness.* London: Longman.

Barber, K. 1991. *I Could Speak until Tomorrow: Oriki, Women and the Past in a Yoruba Town.* Washington DC: Smithsonian Institution Press.

Barber, K. (ed.). 1997. *Readings in African Popular Culture.* Bloomington: Indiana University Press.

Barkan, J. (ed.). 1994. *Beyond Capitalism vs. Socialism in Kenya and Tanzania.* Boulder CO: Lynne Rienner.

Barongo, Y. 1983. *Political Science in Africa.* London: Zed Books.

Barrows, W. 1976. *Grassroots Politics in an African State: Integration and Development in Sierra Leone.* New York: Africana.

Barth, F. (ed.). 1969. *Ethnic Groups and Boundaries.* Boston MA: Little, Brown.

Bates, R. 1983a. *Essays on the Political Economy of Rural Africa.* Cambridge: Cambridge University Press.

Bates, R. 1983b. *Markets and States in Tropical Africa.* Berkeley: University of California Press.

Bates, R. 1989. *Beyond the Miracle of the Market: The Political Economy of Agrarian Development in Kenya.* Cambridge: Cambridge University Press.

Bayart, J.-F. 1979. *L'État au Cameroun.* Paris: Presses de la Fondation Nationale des Sciences Politiques.

Bayart, J.-F. 1986. 'Civil Society in Africa', in P. Chabal (ed.), *Political Domination in Africa: Reflections on the Limits of Power.* Cambridge: Cambridge University Press.

Bayart, J.-F. 1989. *L'Etat en Afrique: la politique du ventre.* Paris: Fayard.

Bayart, J.-F. 2004. *Le gouvernement du monde: une critique politique de la globalisation.* Paris: Fayard.

Bayart, J.-F., S. Ellis and B. Hibou. 1997. *La criminalisation de l'État en Afrique.* Brussels: Complexe.

Baynham, S. 1986. *Military Power and Politics in Black Africa.* London: Croom Helm.

Beattie, J. 1980. 'Representations of the Self in Traditional Africa', *Africa* 50(3), pp. 313–20.

Beckman, B., and G. Adeoti (eds). 2006. *Intellectuals and African Development: Pretensions and Resistance in African Politics.* London: Zed Books.

Behrend, H. 1999. *Alice Lakwena and the Holy Spirits: War in Northern Uganda, 1985–97.* Oxford: James Currey.

Behrend, H., and U. Luig (eds). 1999. *Spirit Possession: Modernity and Power in Africa.* Oxford: James Currey.

Benhabib, S. 1992. *Situating the Self*. New York: Routledge.

Berdal, M., and D. Malone. 2000. *Greed and Grievance: Economic Agendas in Civil Wars*. London: Lynne Rienner.

Berghe, P. van den. 1981. *The Ethnic Phenomenon*. New York: Elsevier.

Berman, B. 1998. 'Ethnicity, Patronage, and the African State', *African Affairs* 97(389), pp. 305–41.

Berman, B., and J. Lonsdale. 1992. *Unhappy Valley: Conflict in Kenya and Africa*, 2 vols. London: James Currey.

Berry, S. 1993. *No Condition is Permanent: The Social Dynamics of Agrarian Change in Sub-Saharan Africa*. Madison: University of Wisconsin Press.

Berry, S. 2001. *Chiefs Know Their Boundaries: Essays on Property, Power and the Past in Asante, 1896–1996*. Oxford: James Currey.

Beveridge, A., and A. Oberschall. 1979. *African Businessmen and Development in Zambia*. Princeton: Princeton University Press.

Bevir, M. 1999. *The Logic of the History of Ideas*. Cambridge: Cambridge University Press.

Bienen, H. 1971. *Tanzania: Party Transformation and Economic Development*. Princeton: Princeton University Press.

Bierschenk, T., and J.-P. Olivier de Sardan. 1998. *Les pouvoirs au village: le Bénin rural entre democratisation et decentralisation*. Paris: Karthala.

Binder, L., et al. 1971. *Crises and Sequences in Political Development*. Princeton: Princeton University Press.

Birnbaum, P. (ed.). 1997. *Sociologie des nationalismes*. Paris: PUF.

Bledsoe, C. 2002. *Contingent Lives: Fertility, Time and Aging in West Africa*. Chicago: Chicago University Press.

Bloch, M., and J. Parry (eds). 1982. *Death and Regeneration of Life*. Cambridge: Cambridge University Press.

Bloch, M., and J. Parry (eds). 1989. *Money and the Morality of Exchange*. Cambridge: Cambridge University Press.

Boone, C. 2003. *Political Topographies of the African State: Territorial Authority and Institutional Choice*. Cambridge: Cambridge University Press.

Boserup, E. 1970. *Women's Role in Economic Development*. New York: St Martin's Press.

Bourdieu, P. 1980. *Le Sens pratique*. Paris: Minuit.

Bourmaud, D. 1997. *La politique en Afrique*. Paris: Montchrestien.

Bowen, M. 2000. *The State against the Peasantry: Rural Struggles in Colonial and Postcolonial Mozambique*. Charlottesville VA: University Press of Virginia.

Bratton, M. 2003. 'Briefing: Islam, Democracy and Public Opinion in Africa', *African Affairs* 102(408), pp. 493–501.

Bratton, M., and N. Van de Walle. 1997. *Democratic Experiments in Africa: Regime Transitions in Comparative Perspective*. Cambridge: Cambridge University Press.

Bratton, M., R. Mattes and E. Gyimah-Boadi. 2005. *Public Opinion, Democracy, and Market Reform in Africa*. Cambridge: Cambridge University Press.

Brecke, P. 2000. *Risk Assessment Models and Early Warning Systems*. Berlin: Wissenschaftszentrum Berlin für Sozialforschung. www.wz-berlin.de/alt/ip/abstracts/p00–302.de.htm.

Cabral, A. 1980. *Unity and Struggle*. London: Heinemann.

Cahen, M. 1994. *Ethnicité politique: pour une lecture réaliste de l'identité*. Paris: L'Harmattan.

Callaghy, T. 1984. *The State–Society Struggle*. New York: Columbia University Press.

Callaghy, T. 1994. 'Civil Society, Democracy, and Economic Change in Africa: A Dissenting Opinion about Resurgent Societies', in S. Harbeson, D. Rothchild and N. Chazan (eds), *Civil Society and the State in Africa*. Boulder CO: Lynne Rienner.

Carré, O. 1982. *L'Islam et l'Etat dans le monde d'aujourd'hui*. Paris: PUF.

Carré, O. (ed.). 1993. *L'islam laïque ou le retour: la grande tradition*. Paris: Armand Colin.

Carrier, J. 1995a. *Gifts and Commodities: Exchange and Western Capitalism since 1700*. London: Routledge.

Carrier, J. 1995b. *Occidentalism: Images of the West*. Oxford: Clarendon Press.

Carroll, D. 1990. *Chinua Achebe*. London: Macmillan.

Chabal, P. 1983. *Amílcar Cabral: Revolutionary Leadership and People's War*. Cambridge: Cambridge University Press; reprint London: Hurst, 2004.

Chabal, P. (ed.). 1986. *Political Domination in Africa: Reflections on the Limits of Power*. Cambridge: Cambridge University Press.

Chabal, P. 1994. *Power in Africa: An Essay in Political Interpretation*. London: Macmillan.

Chabal, P. 1996 'The African Crisis: Context and Interpretation', in R. Werbner and T. Ranger (eds), *Postcolonial Identities in Africa*. London: Zed Books.

Chabal, P. 1997. *Apocalypse Now? A Post-colonial Journey into Africa*, inaugural lecture. London: King's College.

Chabal, P. 1998. 'A Few Reflections on Democracy in Africa', *International Affairs* 74(2).

Chabal, P. 2002. 'The Quest for Good Government and Development in Africa: Is NEPAD the Answer?', *International Affairs* 78(3).

Chabal, P., and J.-P. Daloz. 1999. *Africa Works: Disorder as Political Instrument*. Oxford: James Currey.

Chabal, P., and J.-P. Daloz. 2006. *Culture Troubles: Politics and the Interpretation of Meaning*. London: Hurst.

Chabal, P., U. Engel and L. De Haan (eds). 2007. *African Alternatives*. Leiden: Brill.

Chabal, P., A.M. Gentili and U. Engel. 2005. *Is Violence Inevitable in Africa? Theories of Conflict and Approaches to Conflict Prevention*. Leiden: Brill.

Chabal, P., and N. Vidal. 2007. *Angola: The Weight of History*. London: Hurst.

Chan, S. 2002. *Liberalism, Democracy and Development*. Cambridge: Cambridge University Press.

Chatterjee, P. 1993. *The Nation and its Fragments: Colonial and Postcolonial Histories*. Princeton: Princeton University Press.

Chazan, N., et al. 1988. *Politics and Society in Contemporary Africa*. London: Macmillan.

Cheal, D. 1988. *The Gift Economy*. London: Routledge.

Cheater, A. (ed.) 1999. *The Anthropology of Power: Empowerment, Disempowerment and Changing Structures*. London: Routledge.

Cheru, F. 2002. *African Renaissance: Roadmaps to the Challenge of Globalization*. London: Zed Books.

Chingono, M. 1996. *The State, Violence and Development*. Aldershot: Avebury Press.

Chrétien, J.-P. 1993. *L'invention religieuse en Afrique: histoire et religion en Afrique noire*. Paris: Karthala.

Chrétien, J.-P., and G. Prunier (eds). 1989. *Les ethnies ont une histoire*. Paris: Karthala.

Claessen H., and P. Skalnik. 1981. *The Study of the State*. The Hague: Mouton.

Clapham, C. 1988. *Transformation and Continuity in Revolutionary Ethiopia*. Cambridge: Cambridge University Press.

Clapham, C. 1996. *Africa and the International System: The Politics of State Survival*. Cambridge: Cambridge University Press,.

Clapham, C. 1999. 'Sovereignty and the Third World State', *Political Studies* 47, pp. 522–37.

Clark, J., and D. Gardinier (eds). 1997. *Political Reforms in Francophone Africa*. Boulder CO: Westview Press.

Cohen, A. 1969. *Customs and Politics in Urban Africa*. London: Routledge.

Cohen, A. 1981. *The Politics of Elite Culture*. Berkeley: University of California Press.

Cohen, D., and E.S. Odhiambo. 1992. *Burying SM: The Politics of Knowledge and the Sociology of Power in Africa*. Porstmouth NH: Heinemann.

Coleman, J. 1963. *Nigeria: Background to Nationalism*. Berkeley: University of California Press.

Coleman, J., and C. Rosberg. 1966. *Political Parties and National Integration in Tropical Africa*. Berkeley: University of California Press.

Collier, P. 2007. *The Bottom Billion: Why the Poorest Countries Are Failing and What Can Be Done about It*. Oxford: Oxford University Press.

Collier, P., and A. Hoeffler. 2001. *Greed and Grievance in Civil War*. Washington DC: World Bank.

Collier, R. 1982. *Regimes in Tropical Africa*. Berkeley: University of California Press.

Comaroff, J. 1985. *Body of Power, Spirit of Resistance*. Chicago: Chicago University Press.

Comaroff, J., and J. Comaroff (eds). 1993. *Modernity and Its Malcontents: Ritual and Power in Postcolonial Africa*. Chicago: Chicago University Press.

Comaroff, J., and J. Comaroff. 1997a. *Ethnography and the Historical Imagination*. Boulder CO: Westview Press.

Comaroff, J., and J. Comaroff. 1997b. *Of Revelation and Revolution: The Dialectics of Modernity on a South African Frontier*. Chicago: Chicago University Press.

Comaroff, J., and J. Comaroff (eds). 1999. *Civil Society and the Political Imagination in Africa: Critical Perspectives*. Chicago: Chicago University Press.

Constantin, F., and C. Coulon (eds). 1997. *Religion et transition démocratique en Afrique*. Paris: Karthala.

Coombes, A. 1994. *Reinventing Africa: Museums, Material Culture and Popular Imagination in Late Victorian and Edwardian England*. New Haven: Yale University Press.

Cooper, F. 2002. *Africa since 1940: The Past of the Present*. Cambridge: Cambridge University Press.

Copans, J. 1989. *Les marabouts de l'arachide: la confrérie Mouride et les paysans du Sénégal*. Paris: L'Harmattan.

Copans, J. 1990. *La longue marche de la modernité africaine: savoirs, intellectuels, démocratie*. Paris: Karthala.

Coppet, D. de. 1992. *Understanding Ritual*. London: Routledge.

Coquery-Vidrovitch, C. 1969. 'Recherches sur un mode de production africain', *La Pensée* 144.

Coquery-Vidrovitch, C. 1985. *Afrique noire, permanences et ruptures*. Paris: Payot.

Coronil, F. 1996. 'Beyond Occidentalism: Towards Nonimperial Geo-historical Categories', *Cultural Anthropology* 11(1), pp. 51–87.

Coulon, C. 1981. *Le marabout et le prince: islam et pouvoir au Sénégal*. Paris: Pedone.

Coulon, C. 1983. *Les musulmans et le pouvoir en Afrique noire: religion et contre-culture*. Paris: Karthala.

Coulson, A. 1982. *Tanzania: A Political Economy*. Oxford: Clarendon Press.

Couto, M. 1995. *A Sleepwalking Land* [exerpt], trans. David Brookshaw, *The Literary Review* 38(4), pp. 593–603.

Couto, M. 1990. *Voices Made Night*, trans. David Brookshaw. Oxford: Heinemann.

Couto, M. 1994. *Every Man is a Race*, trans. David Brookshaw. Oxford: Heinemann.

Couto, M. 2001. *Under the Frangipani*, trans. David Brookshaw. London: Serpent's Tail.

Cramer, C. 2006. *Civil War is not a Stupid Thing: Accounting for Violence in Developing Countries*. London: Hurst.

Crook, R., and J. Manor. 1998. *Democracy and Decentralization in South Asia and West Africa: Participation, Accountability and Performance*. Cambridge: Cambridge University Press.

Cruise O'Brien, D. 1971. *The Mourides of Senegal*. Oxford: Oxford University Press.

Cruise O'Brien, D. 2003. *Symbolic Confrontations: Muslims Imagining the State in Africa*. London: Hurst.

Cruise O'Brien, D., et al. (eds). 1989. *Contemporary West African States*. Cambridge: Cambridge University Press.

Crummey, D. 1986. *Banditry, Rebellion and Social Protest in Africa*. London: James Currey.

Crummey, D., and C. Stewart. *Modes of Production in Africa*. London: Sage.

Curtin, P. 1975. *Economic Change in Precolonial Africa*. Madison: University of Wisconsin Press.

Daloz, J.-P. 1998. *Le (non) renouvellement des élites en Afrique subsaharienne*. Paris: Economica.

Daloz, J.-P. 2002. *Elites et représentations politiques: la culture de l'échange inégal au Nigeria*. Bordeaux: Presses Universitaires de Bordeaux.

Daloz, J.-P., and P. Quantin (eds). 1997. *Transitions démocratiques africaines: dynamiques et contraintes (1990–1994)*. Paris: Karthala.

Daneel, M. 1970. *Zionism and Faith Healing in Rhodesia*. The Hague: Mouton.

Darbon, D. (ed.). 1995. *Ethnicité et nation en Afrique du Sud: imageries identitaires et enjeux sociaux*. Paris: Karthala.

Darbon, D., and J. de Gaudusson (eds). 1997. *La création du droit en Afrique*. Paris: Karthala.

de Bruijn, M., and D. Foeken (eds). 2001. *Mobile Africa: Changing Patterns of Movement in Africa and Beyond*. Leiden: Brill.

de Waal, A. 1997. *Famine Crimes*. Oxford: James Currey.

Decalo, S. 1976. *Coups and Army Rule in Africa*. New Haven: Yale University Press.

Delannoi, G., and P.-A. Taguieff (eds). 1991. *Théories du nationalisme: nation, nationalité, ethnicité*. Paris: Kimé.

Déloye, Y. 1997. *Sociologie historique du politique*. Paris: La Découverte.

Denzin, N. 1997. *Intepretative Ethnography: Ethnographic Practices for the Twenty-first Century*. London: Sage.

Deutsch, J.-G., P. Probst and H. Schmidt (eds). 2002. *African Modernities*. Oxford: James Currey.

Devish, R. 1993. *Weaving the Threads: The Khital Gyn-eco-logical Healing Cult among the Yaka*. Chicago: University of Chicago Press.

Dia, M. 1996. *Africa's Management in the 1990s: Reconciling Indigenous and Transplanted Institutions*. Washington DC: World Bank.

Diamond, L. 1988. *Ethnicity and Democracy in Nigeria*. London: Macmillan.

Diamond, L. (ed.). 1993. *Political Culture and Democracy in Developing Countries*. Boulder CO: Lynne Rienner.

Diamond, L., and F. Plattner (eds). 1999. *Democratization in Africa*. Baltimore MD: Johns Hopkins University Press.

Diaw, A. 1994. *Démocratisation et logiques identitaires en acte: l'invention de la politique en Afrique*. Dakar: Codesria.

Dieterlen, G. (ed.). 1973. *La notion de personne en Afrique noire*. Paris: Editions du CNRS.

Downs, R., and S. Reyna. 1988. *Land and Society in Contemporary Africa*. Hanover NH: University Press of New Hampshire.

Dozon, J.-P. 1995. *La cause des prophètes: politique et religion en Afrique contemporaine, suivi de M. Augé, 'La leçon des prophètes'*. Paris: Seuil.

Dozon, J.-P. 2003. *Frères et Sujets: la France et l'Afrique en perspective*. Paris: Flammarion.

Duffield, M. 2001. *Global Governance and the New Wars: The Merging of Development and Security*. London: Zed Books.

Duignan, P., and R. Jackson (eds) 1986. *Politics and Government in African States*. London: Croom Helm.

Dunn, J. 1978. *West African States*. Cambridge: Cambridge University Press.

Dunn, J. 1979. *Western Political Theory in the Face of the Future*. Cambridge: Cambridge University Press.

Duruflé, G. 1988. *L'ajustement structurel en Afrique*. Paris: Karthala.

Easterly, W. 2001. *The Elusive Quest for Growth: Economists' Adventures and Misadventures in the Tropics*. Cambridge MA: MIT Press.

Eboussi Boulaga, F. 1977. *La crise du Muntu: authenticité africaine et philosophie*. Paris: Présence Africaine.

Eisenstadt, S. 1972. *Traditional Patrimonialism and Modern Neopatrimonialism*. London: Sage.

Eisenstadt, S., and R. Lemarchand (eds). 1981. *Political Clientelism, Patronage and Development*. London: Sage.

Ekeh, P. 1975. 'Colonialism and the Two Publics in Africa: A Theoretical Statement', *Comparative Studies in Society and History* 17(1).

Ekeh, P. 1990. 'Social Anthropology and Two Contrasting Uses of Tribalism', *Comparative Studies of Society and History* 32(4).

Ellis, S. 1999. *The Mask of Anarchy: The Destruction of Liberia and the Religious Dimension of an African Civil War*. London: Hurst.

Ellis, S., and G. Ter Haar. 2004. *Worlds of Power: Religious Thought and Political Practice in Africa*. London: Hurst.

Enayet, H. 1982. *Modern Islamic Political Thought*. London: Macmillan.

Englebert, P. 2000. *State Legitimacy and Development in Africa*. Boulder CO: Lynne Rienner.

Enloe, C. 1973. *Ethnic Conflict and Political Development*. Boston MA: Little, Brown.

Eriksen, T. 1993. *Ethnicity and Nationalism: Anthropological Perspectives*. London: Pluto Press.

Evans-Pritchard, E. 1937. *Witchcraft, Oracles and Magic among the Azande*. Oxford: Oxford University Press.

Evans-Pritchard, E. 1940. *The Nuer*. Oxford: Oxford University Press.

Fabian, J. 1983. *Time and the Other: How Anthropology Makes Its Object*. New York: Columbia University Press.

Fabian, J. 1998. *Moments of Freedom: Anthropology and Popular Culture*. Charlottesburg: University of Virginia Press.

Falola, T. 2004. *Nationalism and African Intellectuals*. Rochester NY: University of Rochester Press.

Fanon, F. 1965. *The Wretched of the Earth*. London: McGibbon & Kee.

Fanon, F. 1967a. *Black Skin White Masks*. New York: Grove Press.

Fanon, F. 1967b. *Towards the African Revolution*. New York: Grove Press.

Fardon, R. (ed.). 1990. *Localizing Strategies: The Regionalization of Ethnographic Accounts*. Washington DC: Smithsonian Institution Press.

Fardon, R. (ed.). 1995. *Counterworks*. London: Routledge.

Feierman, S. 1990. *Peasant Intellectuals: Anthropology and History in Tanzania*. Madison: University of Wisconsin Press.

Ferguson, J. 1990. *The Anti-Politics Machine: 'Development', Depoliticization and Bureaucratic Power in Lesotho*. Cambridge: Cambridge University Press.

Ferguson, J. 1999. *Expectations of Modernity: Myths and Meanings of Urban Life on the Zambian Copperbelt*. Berkeley and Los Angeles: University of California Press.

Ferme, M. 2001. *The Underneath of Things: Violence and the Everyday in Sierra Leone*. Berkeley: University of California Press.

Fernandes, J. 1982. *Bwiti: An Ethnography of the Religious Imagination in Africa*. Princeton: Princeton University Press.

Fieldhouse, D. 1986. *Black Africa, 1945–1980*. London: Allen & Unwin.

Finnegan, R. 1988. *Literacy and Orality*. Oxford: Blackwell.

Forrest, J. 2003. *Lineages of State Fragility: Rural Civil Society in Guinea-Bissau*. Oxford: James Currey.

Fortes, M. 1949. *The Web of Kinship among the Tallensi*. Oxford: Oxford University Press.

Fortes, M. 1987. *Religion, Morality and the Person: Essays on Tallensi Religion*, ed. Jack Goody. Cambridge: Cambridge University Press.

Fortes, M., and E. Evans-Pritchard (eds). 1940. *African Political Systems*. Oxford: Oxford University Press.

Foucault, M. 1972. *Power/Knowledge*. New York: Pantheon Books.

Freund, B. 1984. *The Making of Contemporary Africa*. Bloomington and Indianapolis: Indiana University Press.

Gabisirege, S., and S. Babalola. 2001. *Perceptions About the Gacaca Law in Rwanda: Evidence from a Multi-Method Study*, Special Publication no. 19. Baltimore: Johns Hopkins University School of Public Health, Center for Communication Programs.

Galvan, D. 2002. *The State Must Be Our Master of Fire: How Peasants Craft Culturally Sustainable Development in Senegal*. Berkeley: University of California Press.

Gann, L., and P. Duignan. 1969. *Colonialism in Africa, 1870–1960*. Cambridge: Cambridge University Press.

Geertz, C. 1973. *The Interpretation of Cultures: Selected Essays*. New York: Basic Books.

Geertz, C. 1983. *Local Knowledge: Further Essays in Interpretive Anthropology*. New York: Basic Books.

Geertz, C. 2000. *Available Light: Anthropological Reflections on Philosophical Topics*. Princeton: Princeton University Press.

Geffray, C. 1990. *La cause des armes au Mozambique*. Paris: Karthala.

Gellner, E. 1982. 'Relativism and Universals', in M. Hollis, and S. Lukes (eds), *Rationality and Relativism*. Oxford: Basil Blackwell.

Gellner, E. 1983. *Nations and Nationalism*. Oxford: Blackwell.

Gellner, E. 1995. *Anthropology and Politics: Revolutions in the Sacred Grove*. Oxford: Blackwell.

Gellner, E. 1997. Nationalism. London: Weidenfeld & Nicolson.

Geschiere, P. 1996. 'Sorcellerie et politique: les pièges du rapport élite-village', Politique Africaine 63 (October).

Geschiere, P. 1997. The Modernity of Witchcraft: Politics and the Occult in Postcolonial Africa. Charlottesville: University Press of Virginia.

Geschiere, P. 2003. 'On Witch Doctors and Spin Doctors; The Role of 'Experts' in African and American Politics', in P. Pels and B. Meyer (eds), Magic and Modernity: Interfaces of Revelation and Concealment. Stanford: Stanford University Press.

Geschiere, P. 2008. Perils of Belonging: Autochthony, Citizenship and Exclusion in Africa and Europe. Chicago: University of Chicago Press.

Geschiere, P., and J. Gugler (eds). 1998. The Politics of Primary Patriotism, Africa 68 (Special issue).

Geschiere, P., and F. Nyamjoh. 2000. 'Capitalism and Autochthony: The Seesaw of Mobility and Belonging', Public Culture 12.

Giddens, A. 1984. The Constitution of Society: Outline of a Theory of Structuration. Berkeley: University of California Press.

Giddens, A. 1991. Modernity and Self-Identity. Stanford CA: Stanford University Press.

Gifford, P., and W. Louis. 1982. The Transfer of Power in Africa. New Haven: Yale University Press.

Gilroy, P. 1993. The Black Atlantic: Modernity and Double Consciousness. London: Verso.

Gladwin, C. (ed.). 1991. Structural Adjustment and African Women Farmers. Gainesville: University of Florida Press.

Gledhill, J. 2000. Power and Its Disguises: Anthropological Perspectives on Politics. London: Pluto Press.

Gluckman, M. 1960. Custom and Conflict in Africa. Oxford: Blackwell.

Gluckman, M. 1965. Politics, Law and Ritual in Tribal Society. Oxford: Blackwell.

Godelier, M. 1977. Perspectives in Marxist Anthropology. Cambridge: Cambridge University Press.

Godelier, M. 1999. The Enigma of the Gift. Cambridge: Polity Press.

Goetz, A.M., and S. Hassim (eds). 2003. No Shortcuts to Power: African Women in Politics and Policy Making. London: Zed Books.

Goody, E. 1982. Parenthood and Social Reproduction. Cambridge: Cambridge University Press.

Goody, J. 1971. Technology, Tradition and the State in Africa. Oxford: Oxford University Press.

Goody, J. 1976. Production and Reproduction: A Comparative Study of the Domestic Domain. Cambridge: Cambridge University Press.

Gottlieb, A. 1992. Under the Kapok Tree: Identity and Difference in Beng Thought. Bloomington: Indiana University Press.

Gregory, C. 1982. Gifts and Commodities. New York: Academic Press.

Gregory, C. 1997. Savage Money. Amsterdam: Harwood Academic Press.

Grosh, B. 1991. *Public Enterprise in Kenya: What Works, What Doesn't and Why.* Boulder CO: Lynne Rienner.

Gueye, A. 2001. *Les intellectuals africains en France.* Paris: L'Harmattan.

Gulliver, P. (ed.). 1969. *Tradition and Transition in East Africa: Studies of the Tribal Element in the Modern Era.* London: Routledge & Kegan Paul.

Gupta, A., and J. Ferguson (eds). 1997. *Culture, Power and Place: Explorations in Critical Anthropology.* Durham NC: Duke University Press.

Gutkind, P., and I. Wallerstein (eds). 1976. *The Political Economy of Contemporary Africa.* Beverly Hills: Sage.

Guyer, J. 1995. 'Wealth in People as Wealth in Knowledge: Accumulation and Composition in Equatorial Africa', *Journal of African History* 36, pp. 121–40.

Guyer, J. (ed.). 1995. *Money Matters: Instability, Values and Social Payments in the Modern History of West African Communities.* Portsmouth NH: Heinemann.

Hannerz, U. 1992. *Cultural Complexity: Studies in the Social Organization of Meaning.* New York: Columbia University Press.

Hannerz, U. 1996. *Transnational Connections: Culture, People, Places.* New York: Routledge.

Harbeson, J.W., D. Rothchild and N. Chazan (eds). 1994. *Civil Society and the State in Africa.* Boulder CO: Lynne Rienner.

Hart, K. 1980. *The Political Economy of West African Agriculture.* Cambridge: Cambridge University Press.

Hayward. H. 1986. *Elections in Independent Africa.* Boulder CO: Westview Press.

Hecht, D., and A.M. Simone. 1994. *Invisible Governance: The Art of African Micro-politics.* New York: Autonomedia.

Heesterman, J. 1985. *The Inner Conflict of Traditions.* Chicago: Chicago University Press.

Heidenheimer. A. 1978. *Political Corruption: Readings in Comparative Analysis.* New Brunswick NJ: Transaction.

Held, D., et al. (eds). 1999. *Global Transformations: Politics, Economics and Culture.* Cambridge: Polity Press.

Herbst, J. 2000. *States and Power in Africa: Comparative Lessons in Authority and Control.* Princeton NJ: Princeton University Press.

Herskovits, M. 1938. *Acculturation: The Study of Culture Contact.* New York: Augustin.

Heusch, L. de. 1982. *The Drunken King or the Origins of the State.* Bloomington: Indiana University Press.

Heusch, L. de. 1985. *Sacrifice in Africa.* Bloomington: Indiana University Press.

Higginson, J. 1989. *A Working Class in the Making: Belgian Colonial Labor Policy, Private Entereprise and the African Mineworkers, 1907–1951.* Madison: University of Wisconsin Press.

Hill, P. 1963. *The Migrant Cocoa Farmers of Southern Ghana.* Cambridge: Cambridge University Press.

Hill. P. 1982. *Dry Grain Farming Families: Hausaland (Nigeria) and Karnataka (India) Compared.* Cambridge: Cambridge University Press.

Hirschman, A. 1970. *Exit, Voice and Loyalty*. Cambridge MA: Harvard University Press.

Hobsbawn, E., and T. Ranger (eds). 1983. *The Invention of Tradition*. Cambridge: Cambridge University Press.

Hodder-Williams, R. 1984. *An Introduction to the Politics of Tropical Africa*. London: Allen & Unwin.

Hodges, T. 2001. *Angola from Afro-Stalinism to Petro-Diamond Capitalism*. Oxford: James Currey.

Hodgkin, T. 1956. *Nationalism in Colonial Africa*. London: Muller.

Honwana, A. 2005. *Child Soldiers in Africa*. Philadelphia: University of Pennsylvania Press.

Hopkins, A. 1973. *An Economic History of West Africa*. London: Longman.

Hountondji, P. 1976. *Sur la 'philosophie africaine': critique de l'ethnophilosophie*. Paris: Maspéro.

Humphrey, C., and S. Hugh-Jones (eds). 1992. *Barter, Exchange and Value: An Anthropological Approach*. Cambridge: Cambridge University Press.

Huntington, S. 1991. *The Third Wave: Democratization in the Late Twentieth Century*. Norman: University of Oklahoma Press.

Huntington, S. 1997. *The Clash of Civilizations and the Re-making of the World Order*. New York: Simon & Schuster.

Hutchinson, S. 1996. *Nuer Dilemmas: Coping with Money, War and the State*. Berkeley and Los Angeles: University of California Press.

Hydén, G. 1980. *Beyond Ujamaa in Tanzania: Underdevelopment and an Uncaptured Peasantry*. Berkeley and Los Angeles: University of California Press.

Hydén, G. 1997. 'Civil Society, Social Capital and Development: Dissection of a Complex Discourse', *Studies in Comparative International Development* 32(1), pp. 3–30.

Hydén, G. 2006. *African Politics in Comparative Perspective*. Cambridge: Cambridge University Press.

Iliffe, J. 1979. *A Modern History of Tanzania*. Cambridge: Cambridge University Press.

Iliffe, J. 1983. *The Emergence of African Capitalism*. London: Macmillan.

Iliffe, J. 1987. *The African Poor*. Cambridge: Cambridge University Press.

Iliffe, J. 1995. *Africans: The History of a Continent*. Cambridge: Cambridge University Press.

Iliffe, J. 2005. *Honour in African History*. Cambridge: Cambridge University Press.

Iliffe, J. 2006. *The African AIDS Epidemic: A History*. Oxford: James Currey.

Inglehart, R., and C. Welzel. 2005. *Modernization, Cultural Change and Democracy: The Human Development Sequence*. Cambridge: Cambridge University Press.

Iniesta, F. 1995. *L'univers africain: approche historique des cultures noires*. Paris: L'Harmattan.

Inkeles, A., and D. Smith. 1974. *Becoming Modern: Individual Change in Six Developing Countries*. London: Heinemann.

Isaacman, A. 1976. *The Tradition of Resistance in Mozambique*. Berkeley: University of California Press.

Izard, M. 1985. *Gens du pouvoir, gens de la terre: les institutions politiques de l'ancien royaume du Yatenga*. Cambridge: Cambridge University Press.

Jackson, M., and I. Karp (eds). 1990. *Personhood and Agency: The Experience of Self and Other in African Cultures*. Washington DC: Smithsonian Institution Press.

Jackson, R. 1990. *Quasi-states: Sovereignty, International Relations and the Third World*. Cambridge: Cambridge University Press.

Jackson, R., and C. Rosberg. 1982. *Personal Rule in Black Africa*. Berkeley: University of California Press.

Jewsiewicki, B., and D. Newbury. 1986. *African Historiographies*. Beverley Hills CA: Sage.

Johnston, M. 2005. *Syndromes of Corruption: Wealth, Power and Democracy*. Cambridge: Cambridge University Press.

Joseph, R. 1987. *Democracy and Prebendal Politics in Nigeria*. Cambridge: Cambridge University Press.

Kaarsholm, P. (ed.). 2006. *Violence, Political Culture and Development in Africa*. Oxford: James Currey.

Kabou, A. 1991. *Et si l'Afrique refusait le développement?* Paris: L'Harmattan.

Kahn, J., and J. Llobera (eds). 1981. *The Anthropology of Pre-capitalist Societies*. London: Macmillan.

Kane, O., and J.-L. Triaud (eds). 1998. *Islam et islamismes au sud du Sahara*. Paris: Karthala.

Kaplan, R. 1994. 'The Coming Anarchy', *Atlantic Monthly* 273(2), pp. 44–76.

Kaplan, R. 1997. *The Ends of the Earth: A Journey to the Frontiers of Anarchy*. New York: Random House.

Kasfir, N. 1967. *The Shrinking Political Arena*. Berkeley: University of California Press.

Kasfir, N. (ed.). 1984. *State and Class in Africa*. London: Frank Cass.

Kasfir, N. (ed.). 1998. *Civil Society and Democracy in Africa: Critical Perspectives*. London: Frank Cass.

Kedourie, E. (ed.). 1993. *Nationalism in Asia and Africa*, 4th edn. Oxford: Blackwell.

Kelsall, T. 2004. *Contentious Politics and the Self: A Tanzanian Case Study*. Research Report no. 129. Uppsala: Nordiska Afrikainstitutet.

Kennedy, P. 1988. *African Capitalism: The Struggle for Ascendancy*. Cambridge: Cambridge University Press.

Kenyatta, J. 1938. *Facing Mount Kenya*. London: Secker & Warburg.

Kenyatta, J. 1968. *Suffering without Bitterness*. Nairobi: East African Publishing House.

Kirk-Greene, A. 1974. *Mutumin Kirkii: The Concept of the Good Man in Hausa*. Bloomington: Indiana University Press.

Kitching, G. 1980. *Class and Economic Change in Kenya*. New Haven: Yale University Press.

Kjaer, A. 2004. *Governance*. Cambridge: Polity Press.

Klein, M. 1998. *Slavery and Colonial Rule in French West Africa*. Cambridge: Cambridge University Press.

Konings, P. 2001. 'Mobility and Exclusion: Conflict between Autochthons and Allochtons during Political Liberalization in Cameroon', in M. de Bruijn and D. Foeken (eds), *Mobile Africa: Changing Patterns of Movement in Africa and Beyond*. Leiden: Brill.

Kopytoff, I. (ed.). 1987. *The African Frontier: The Reproduction of Traditional African Societies*. Bloomington: Indiana University Press.

Kourouma, A. 1970. *Les soleils des indépendances*. Paris: Seuil.

Kourouma, A. 1998. *En attendant le vote des bêtes sauvages*. Paris: Seuil.

Kuba, R., and C. Lentz (eds). 2006. *Land and the Politics of Belonging in West Africa*. Leiden: Brill, 2006.

Kuper, A. 1988. *The Invention of Primitive Society: Transformations of an Illusion*. London: Routledge.

Laitin, D. 1986. *Hegemony and Culture: Politics and Religious Change among the Yoruba*. Chicago: Chicago University Press.

Laitin, D. 1992. *Language Repertoires and State Construction in Africa*. Cambridge: Cambridge University Press

Lan, D. 1985. *Guns and Rain: Guerrillas and Spirit Mediums in the Zimbabwe War of Independence*. Berkeley and Los Angeles: University of California Press.

Lassiter, J. 2001. 'African Culture and Personality: Bad Social Science, Effective Social Activism or a Call to Reinvent Ethnology?', *African Studies Quarterly* 3.

Le Vine, V. 1975. *Political Corruption: The Ghana Case*. Stanford: Hoover Institution Press.

Lemarchand, R. 1994. *Ethnocide as Discourse and Practice*. Cambridge: Cambridge University Press.

Lentz, C., and P. Nugent. 2000. *Ethnicity in Ghana: The Limits of Invention*. London: Macmillan.

Leonard, D., and S. Strauss. 2003. *Africa's Stalled Development: International Causes and Cures*. Boulder CO: Lynne Rienner.

Lévi-Strauss, C. 1955. *Tristes Tropiques*. Paris: Plon.

LeVine, R. 1966. *Dreams and Deeds: Achievement Motivation in Nigeria*. Chicago: Chicago University Press.

Lévy-Bruhl, L. 1960. *La mentalité primitive*. Paris: PUF.

Leys, C. 1975. *Underdevelopment in Kenya*. London: Heinemann.

Leys, C. 1996. *The Rise and Fall of Development Theory*. Oxford: James Currey.

Lijphart, A. 1977. *Democracy in Plural Societies: A Comparative Exploration*. New Haven: Yale University Press.

Liniger-Goumaz. M. 1989. *Small is Not Always Beautiful*. London: Hurst.

Little, K. 1965. *West African Urbanization: A Study of Voluntary Organization in Social Change*. Cambridge: Cambridge University Press.

Lloyd, P. 1966. *The New Elites of Tropical Africa*. Oxford: Oxford University Press.

Lodge, T. 2006. *Mandela: A Critical Life*. Oxford: Oxford University Press.

Lonsdale, J. 1981. 'States and Social Processes in Africa', *African Studies Review* 24, pp. 2–3.

Lonsdale, J. 1989. 'Africa's Pasts in Africa's Future', *Canadian Journal of African Studies* 23(1).

Lonsdale, J. 1992. 'The Moral Economy of Mau Mau', in J. Lonsdale and B. Berman, *Unhappy Valley: Conflict in Kenya and Africa*. London: James Currey.

Lonsdale, J. 1994. 'Moral Ethnicity and Political Tribalism', in P. Kaarsholm and J. Hultin (eds), *Inventions and Boundaries: Historical and Anthropological Approaches to the Study of Ethnicity and Nationalism*. Papers from the Researcher Training Course held at Sandbjerg Manor, 23–29 May 1993. Roskilde: IDS Roskilde University.

Lonsdale, J. 1995. 'Moral Ethnicity, Ethnic Nationalism and Political Tribalism: The Case of the Kikuyu', in P. Meyns (ed.), *Staat und Gesellschaft in Afrika: Erosions- und Reformprozesse*. Hamburg: Lit Verlag.

Lonsdale, J. 2003. 'Moral and Political Argument in Kenya', in B. Berman, D. Eyoh and W. Kymlicka (eds), *Ethnicity and Democracy in Africa*. Oxford: James Currey.

Lonsdale, J. 2008. 'Soil, Work, Civilisation, and Citizenship in Kenya', *Journal of Eastern African Studies* 2(2), pp. 305–14.

Lubkemann, S. 2008. *Culture in Chaos: An Anthropology of the Social Condition in War*. Chicago: Chicago University Press.

Luckham, R. 1971. *The Nigerian Military*. Cambridge: Cambridge University Press.

MacGaffey, J. 1987. *Entrepeneurs and Parasites: The Struggle for Indigenous Capitalism in Zaïre*. Cambridge: Cambridge University Press.

MacGaffey, J., and R. Bazenguissa-Ganga. 2000. *Congo–Paris: Transnational Traders on the Margins of the Law*. Oxford: James Currey.

Malkki, L. 1995. *Purity and Exile: Violence, Memory and National Cosmology among Hutu Refugees in Tanzania*. Chicago: Chicago University Press.

Mama, A. 1996. *Women Studies and Studies of Women in Africa during the 1990s*. Dakar: Codesria.

Mamdani, M. 1976. *Politics and Class Formation in Uganda*. London: Heinemann.

Mamdani, M. 1993. *The Intelligentsia, the State and Social Movements in Africa*. Dakar: Codesria.

Mamdani, M. 1996. *Citizen and Subject: Contemporary Africa and the Legacy of Late Colonialism*. Princeton: Princeton University Press.

Manning, P. 1990. *Slavery and African Life: Occidental, Oriental and African Slave Trades*. Cambridge: Cambridge University Press.

Manning, P. 1999. *Francophone Sub-Saharan Africa 1880–1995*, 2nd edn. Cambridge: Cambridge University Press.

Marie, A. (ed.). 1997. *L'Afrique des individus*. Paris: Karthala.

Markakis, J. 1987. *National and Class Conflict in the Horn of Africa*. Cambridge: Cambridge University Press.

Markovitz, I. 1977. *Power and Class in Africa*. Englewoods Cliffs NJ: Prentice-Hall.

Markovitz, I. 1987. *Studies in Power and Class in Africa*. Oxford: Oxford University Press.

Marris, P., and A. Somerset. 1971. *African Businessmen: A Study of Entrepreneurship and Development in Kenya*. London: Routledge & Kegan Paul.

Marseille, J. 1984. *Empire colonial et capitalisme français*. Paris: Albin Michel.

Martin, D.-C. 1988. *Tanzanie: l'invention d'une culture politique*. Paris: Karthala.

Martin, D.-C. 1992. 'La découverte des cultures politiques: esquisse d'une approche comparatiste à partir des experiences africaines', *Les Cahiers du CERI* 2.

Martin, P. 1995. *Leisure and Society in Colonial Brazzaville*. Cambridge: Cambridge University Press.

Mazrui, A. (ed.). 1993. *General History of Africa: Africa since 1935*. Berkeley and Los Angeles: University of California Press.

Mbembe, A. 1985. *Les jeunes et l'ordre politique en Afrique noire*. Paris: L'Harmattan.

Mbembe, A. 1988. *Afriques indociles*. Paris: Karthala

Mbembe, A. 2000. *De la postcolonie: essai sur l'imagination politique dans l'Afrique contemporaine*. Paris: Karthala.

McCulloch, J. 1995. *Colonial Psychiatry and the 'African Mind'*. Cambridge: Cambridge University Press.

McIntosh, S.K. (ed.). 1999. *Beyond Chiefdoms: Pathways to Complexity in Africa*. Cambridge: Cambridge University Press.

Médard, J.-F. 1982. 'The Underdeveloped State in Tropical Africa: Political Clientelism or Neo-Patrimonialism?', in C. Clapham (ed.), *Private Patronage and Public Power: Political Clientelism in the Modern State*. London: Frances Pinter.

Médard, J.-F. (ed.). 1991. *Etats d'Afrique noire: formations, mécanismes, crises*. Paris: Karthala.

Médard, J.-F. 1992. 'Le "Big Man" en Afrique: esquisse d'analyse du politicien entrepreneur', *L'Année sociologique*.

Meillassoux, C. 1981. *Maidens, Meal and Money: Capitalism and the Domestic Community*. Cambridge: Cambridge University Press.

Meillassoux, C., and C. Messiant (eds). 1991. *Génie social et manipulations culturelles en Afrique du Sud*. Paris: Arcantère.

Melucci, A. 1996. *The Playing Self: Person and Meaning in the Planetary Society*. Cambridge: Cambridge University Press.

Meyer, B., and P. Geschiere (eds). 1999. *Globalization and Identity: Dialectics of Flow and Closure*. Oxford: Blackwell.

Miano, L. 2005. *L'intérieur de la nuit*. Paris: Plon.

Middleton, J. (ed.). 1997. *Encyclopedia of Africa South of the Sahara*. New York: Scribner's.

Migdal, J. 1988. *Strong Societies and Weak States: State–Society Relations and State Capabilities in the Third World*. Princeton: Princeton University Press.

Mikell, G. (ed.). 1997. *African Feminism*. Philadelphia: University of Pennsylvania Press.

Miller, C. 1990. *Theories of Africans: Francophone Literature and Anthropology in Africa*. Chicago: University of Chicago Press.

Miller, D (ed.). 1995. *Worlds Apart: Modernity through the Prism of the Local*. London: Routledge.

Mitchell, C. 1987. *Cities, Society and Social Perception: A Central African Perspective.* Oxford: Clarendon Press.

Mittelman, J. 2000. *The Globalization Syndrome: Transformation and Renaissance.* Princeton: Princeton University Press.

Mkandawire, T. (ed.). 2006. *African Intellectuals: Rethinking Politics, Language, Gender and Development.* London: Zed Books.

Mkandawire, T., and C. Soludo. 1999. *Between Liberalisation and Oppression: The Politics of Structural Adjustment in Africa.* Dakar: Codesria Press.

Monga, C. 1998. *The Anthropology of Anger: Civil Society and Democracy in Africa.* Boulder CO: Lynne Rienner.

Moore, H., and T. Sanders (eds). 2001. *Magical Interpretations, Material Realities: Modernity, Witchcraft and the Occult in Postcolonial Africa.* London: Routledge.

Moore, S.F. 1994. *Anthropology and Africa: Changing Perspectives on a Changing Scene.* Charlottesville, University Press of Virginia.

Moran, M. 2006. *Liberia: The Violence of Democracy.* Philadelphia: University of Pennsylvania Press.

Mosely Lesch, A. 1999. *The Sudan: Contested National Identities.* Oxford: James Currey.

Moshi, L., and A. Osman (eds). 2008. *Democracy and Culture: An African Perspective.* Lagos: Adonis & Abbey.

Mudimbe, V.Y. 1988. *The Invention of Africa: Gnosis, Philosophy and the Order of Knowledge.* Bloomington: Indiana University Press.

Mudimbe, V.Y. 1997. *Tales of Faith: Religion as Political Performance in Central Africa.* London: Athlone Press.

Museveni, Y. 1997. *Sowing the Mustard Seed: The Struggles for Freedom and Democracy in Uganda.* London: Macmillan.

Myers, F. (ed.). 2001. *The Empire of Things: Regimes of Value and Material Culture.* Oxford: James Currey.

Ngugi wa Thiong'o. 1982. *Writers in Politics.* London: Heinemann.

Ngugi wa Thiong'o. 1985. *Barrel of a Pen.* London: New Beacon.

Nicolas, G. 1986. *Don rituel et échange marchand dans une société sahélienne.* Paris: Institut d'Ethnologie.

Niehaus, I., E. Mohlala and K. Shokane. 2001. *Witchcraft, Power and Politics.* London: Pluto Press.

Nkrumah, K. 1961. *I Speak of Freedom.* New York: Praeger.

Nordstrom, C. 1997. *A Different Kind of War Story.* Philadelphia: University of Pennsylvania Press.

Nordstrom, C. 2007. *Global Outlaws: Crime, Money, and Power in the Contemporary World.* Berkeley: University of California Press.

Nugent, P. 2004. *Africa since Independence: A Comparative History.* London: Palgrave Macmillan.

Nyerere, J. 1973. *Freedom and Development.* Dar es Salaam: Oxford University Press.

Olivier de Sardan, J.-P. 1992. 'Occultism and the Ethnographic "I": The Exoticizing of Magic from Durkheim to "Postmodern" Anthropology', *Critique of Anthropology* 12(1), pp. 5–25.

Olivier de Sardan, J.-P. 1999. 'A Moral Economy of Corruption', *Journal of Modern African Studies* 37(1), pp. 25–52.

Oloka-Onyango, J. 2001. *Constitutionalism in Africa: Creating Opportunities, Facing Challenges.* Kampala: Fountain Publishers.

Olowu, D. 1999. *Governance and Democratization in West Africa.* Dakar: Codesria.

Olukoshi, A. (ed.). 1998. *The Politics of Opposition in Contemporary Africa.* Uppsala: Nordisk Afrikainstitutet.

Onimode, B. 1992. *A Future for Africa: Beyond the Politics of Structural Adjustment.* London: Earthscan.

Osabu-kle, D. 2000. *Compatible Cultural Democracy: The Key to Development in Africa.* Peterborough ON: Broadview Press.

Osman, A. 2007. *Governance and Internal Wars in Sub-saharan Africa: Exploring the Relationship.* Lagos: Adonis & Abbey.

Otayek, R. 2000. *Identité et démocratie dans un monde global.* Paris: Presses de Sciences Politiques.

Oyugi, W., et al. 1988. *Democratic Theory and Practice in Africa.* London: James Currey.

Parkin, D., and D. Nyamwaya (eds). 1987. *Transformations of African Marriage.* Manchester: Manchester University Press.

Parpart, J., and K. Staudt (eds). 1989. *Women and the State in Africa.* Boulder CO: Lynne Rienner.

Parry, J., and M. Bloch 1989. *Money and the Morality of Exchange.* Cambridge: Cambridge University Press.

Paulme, D. (ed.). 1971. *Classes et associations d'age en Afrique de l'Ouest.* Paris: Plon.

Peel, J. 1983. *Ijeshas and Nigerians.* Cambridge: Cambridge University Press.

Pels, P., and B. Meyer (eds). 2003. *Magic and Modernity: Interfaces of Revelation and Concealment.* Stanford: Stanford University Press.

Piot, C. 1999. *Remotely Global: Village Modernity in West Africa.* Chicago: University of Chicago Press.

Pitkin, H. 1972. *The Concept of Representation.* Berkeley and Los Angeles: University of California Press.

Posner, D. 2005. *Institutions and Ethnic Politics in Africa.* Cambridge: Cambridge University Press.

Poutignac, P., and J. Streiff-Fenard (eds). 1995. *Théories de l'ethnicité.* Paris: PUF.

Price, R. 1975. *Society and Bureaucracy in Contemporary Ghana.* Berkeley and Los Angeles: University of California Press.

Prunier, G. 1995. *The Rwanda Crisis: History of a Genocide, 1959–1994.* London: Hurst.

Quantin, P. (ed.). 1994. *L'Afrique politique 1994: vue sur la démocratisation à marée basse.* Paris/Talence: Karthala/CEAN.

Ranger, T. 1985. *The Invention of Tribalism in Zimbabwe.* Gweru: Mambo Press.

Ranger, T. 1999. *Voices from the Rocks: Nature, Culture and History in Matopos Hills of Zimbabwe.* Oxford: James Currey.

Ranger, T., and R. Werbner (eds). 1996. *Postcolonial Identities in Africa.* London: Zed Books.

Rathbone, R. 2000. *Nkrumah and the Chiefs: The Politics of Chieftaincy in Ghana 1951–60*. Oxford: James Currey.

Ravenhill, J. 1986. *Africa in Economic Crisis*. New York: Columbia University Press.

Ray, B. 1991. *Myth, Ritual and Kingship in Buganda*. Oxford: Oxford University Press.

Reno, W. 1995. *Corruption and State Politics in Sierra Leone*. Cambridge: Cambridge University Press.

Reno, W. 2000. *Warlord Politics and African States*. Boulder CO: Lynne Rienner.

Reynolds, B. 1963. *Magic, Divination and Witchcraft among the Barotse of Northern Rhodesia*. London: Chatto & Windus.

Richards, A. 1982. *Chisungu: A Girl's Initiation Ceremony among the Bemba of Zambia*. London: Tavistock.

Richards, P. 1985. *Indigenous Agricultural Revolution*. London: Allen & Unwin.

Richards, P. 1996. *Fighting for the Rain Forest: War, Youth and Resources in Sierra Leone*. Oxford: James Currey.

Richards, P. 1998. 'Sur la nouvelle violence politique en Afrique: le sectarisme séculier en Sierra Leone', *Politique Africaine* 70 (June).

Richards, P. (ed.). 2004. *No Peace, No War: An Anthropology of Contemporary Armed Conflicts*. Oxford: James Currey.

Riesman, P. 1986. 'The Person and the Life Cycle in African Social Life and Thought', *African Studies Review* 29(2), pp. 71–138.

Riesman, P. 1992. *First Find Your Child a Good Mother: The Construction of Self in Two African Communities*. New Brunswick NJ: Rutgers University Press.

Riggs, F. 1998. 'The Modernity of Ethnic Identity and Conflict', *International Political Science Review* 19(3), pp. 269–88.

Rimmer, D. 1984. *The Economies of West Africa*. London: Weidenfeld & Nicolson.

Robert, A.-C. 2004. *L'Afrique au secours de l'Occident*, with a preface by Boubacar Boris Diop. Paris: Editions de l'Atelier.

Robinson, D. 2000. *Paths of Accommodation: Muslim Societies and French Colonial Authorities in Senegal and Mauritania, 1880–1920*. Oxford: James Currey.

Rodney, W. 1972. *How Europe Underdeveloped Africa*. London: Bogle L'Overture.

Rosny, E. de. 1981. *Les yeux de ma chèvre*. Paris: Plon.

Rothchild, D., and N. Chazan. 1988. *The Precarious Balance: State and Society in Africa*. Boulder CO: Westview Press.

Rothchild, D., and V. Olorunsola (eds). 1982. *State versus Ethnic Claims: African Policy Dilemmas*. Boulder CO: Westview Press.

Said, E. 1978. *Orientalism*. New York: Pantheon.

Said, E. 1993. *Culture and Imperialism*. New York: Vintage Books.

Sambanis, N. 2001. 'Do Ethnic and Nonethnic Conflicts Have the Same Causes?' *Journal of Conflict Resolution* 45(3).

Sandbrook, R. 1982. *The Politics of Basic Needs: Urban Aspects of Assaulting Poverty in Africa*. London: Heinemann.

Sandbrook, R. 1985. *The Politics of Africa's Economic Stagnation*. Cambridge: Cambridge University Press.

Sandbrook, R. 2000. *Closing the Circle: Democratisation and Development in Africa.* London: Zed Books.

Sandbrook, R., and R. Cohen. 1975. *The Development of an African Working Class.* London: Longman.

Saro-Wiwa, K. 1991. *Similia: Essays on Anomic Nigeria.* London: Saros.

Schatzberg, M. 1988. *The Dialectics of Oppression in Zaire.* Bloomington: Indiana University Press.

Schatzberg, M. 1993. 'Power, Legitimacy and "Democratization" in Africa', *Africa* 63.

Schatzberg, M. 2001. *Political Legitimacy in Middle Africa: Father, Family, Food.* Indianapolis: Indiana University Press.

Schrift, A. 1997. *The Logic of the Gift.* London: Routledge.

Schumaker, L. 2001. *Africanizing Anthropology: Fieldwork, Networks, and the Making of Cultural Knowledge in Central Africa.* Durham NC: Duke University Press.

Semboja, J., and O. Therkildsen (eds). 1995. *Service Provision under Stress in East Africa.* London: James Currey.

Sen, A. 1983. *Poverty and Famines.* Oxford: Oxford University Press.

Sen, A. 1999. *Development as Freedom.* New York: Knopf.

Shankman, P. 1984. 'The Thick and the Thin: On the Interpretive Theoretical Program of Clifford Geertz', *Current Anthropology* 25(3), pp. 261–79.

Shaw, R. 1997. 'The Production of Witchcraft/Witchcraft as Production: Memory, Modernity, and the Slave Trade in Sierra Leone', *American Ethnologist* 24(4), pp. 856–76.

Sheldon, K. 2002. *Pounders of Grain: A History of Women, Work and Politics in Mozambique.* Portsmouth NH: Heinemann.

Shipton, P. 1989. *Bitter Money: Cultural Economy and Some African Meanings of Forbidden Commodities.* Washington DC: American Anthropological Association.

Shivji, I. 1976. *Class Struggles in Tanzania.* London: Heinemann.

Shivji, I. (ed.). 1986. *The State and the Working People in Tanzania.* Dakar: Codesria.

Shweder, R.A., and R. LeVine (eds). 1984. *Culture Theory: Essays on Mind, Self and Emotion.* Cambridge: Cambridge University Press.

Singleton, M. 2004. *Critique de l'ethnocentrisme.* Paris: Parangon.

Smith, S. 2003. *Négrologie: pourquoi l'Afrique meurt.* Paris: Calmann-Lévy.

Soyinka, W. 1976. *Myth, Literature and the African World.* Cambridge: Cambridge University Press.

Soyinka, W. 1996. *The Open Sore of a Continent: A Personal Narrative of the Nigerian Crisis.* Oxford: Oxford University Press.

Stilwell, S. 2004. *Paradoxes of Power: The Kano 'Mamluks' and Male Royal Slavery in the Sokoto Caliphate, 1804–1903.* Portsmouth NH: Heinemann.

Stocking, G. 1968. *Race, Culture and Evolution: Essays in the History of Anthropology.* New York: Free Press.

Stocking, G. (ed.). 1991. *Colonial Situations: Essays on the Contextualization of Ethnographic Knowledge.* Madison: University of Wisconsin Press.

Stoller, P. 1995. *Embodying Colonial Memories: Spirit Possession, Power and the Hauka in West Africa.* London: Routledge.

Strathern, M. 1988. *The Gender of the Gift: Problems with Women and Problems with Society in Melanesia*. Berkeley and Los Angeles: University of California Press.

Suret-Canale, J. 1988. *Essays on African History*. London: Hurst.

Swanson, R. 1985. *Gourmantché Ethnoanthropology: A Theory of Human Being*. New York: University Press of America.

Tambiah, S. 1985. *Culture, Thought and Social Action: An Anthropological Perspective*. Cambridge MA: Harvard University Press.

Tanberg Hansen, K., and M. Vaa. 2003. *Reconsidering Informality: Perspectives from Urban Africa*. Uppsala: Nordic Africa Institute Press.

Tangri, R. 1985. *Politics in Sub-Saharan Africa*. London: James Currey.

Tangri, R. 1999. *The Politics of Patronage in Africa: Parastatals, Privatization and Private Enterprise*. Oxford: James Currey.

Taylor, C. 1994. *Multiculturalism: Examining the Politics of Recognition*. Princeton: Princeton University Press.

Taylor, I., and P. Williams (eds). 2004. *Africa in International Politics: External Involvement on the Continent*. London: Routledge.

Ter Haar, G. 1992. *Spirit of Africa: The Healing Ministry of Archbishop Milingo of Zambia*. London: Hurst.

Terray, E. 1972. *Marxism and Primitive Societies*. New York: Monthly Review Press.

Terray, E. 1986. 'Le climatiseur et la véranda', in *Afrique plurielle, Afrique actuelle: Hommage à Georges Balandier*. Paris: Karthala.

Theobald, R. 1990. *Corruption, Development and Underdevelopment*. London: Macmillan.

Todorov, T. 1989. *Nous et les autres: la réflexion française sur la diversité humaine*. Paris: Seuil.

Tonkin, E. 1995. *Narrating our Pasts: The Social Construction of Oral History*. Cambridge: Cambridge University Press.

Tordoff, W. 1984. *Government and Politics in Africa*. Bloomington: Indiana University Press.

Trager, L. 2001. *Yoruba Hometowns: Community, Identity and Development in Nigeria*. Boulder CO: Lynne Rienner.

Tripp, A.M. 1997. *Women and Politics in Uganda*. Madison: University of Wisconsin Press.

Turner, E. 1992. *Experiencing Rituals: A New Interpretation of African Healing*. Philadelphia: University of Pennsylvania Press.

Turner, V. 1986. *The Anthropology of Performance*. New York: PAJ Publications.

UNAIDS. 2002. *Report on the Global HIV/AIDS Epidemic*. Geneva: UNAIDS.

Vail, L. 1989. *The Creation of Tribalism in Southern Africa*. Oxford: James Currey.

Vaillant, J. 1990. *Black, French and African: A Life of Léopold Sédar Senghor*. Cambridge MA: Harvard University Press.

van de Walle, N. 2001. *African Economies and the Politics of Permanent Crisis, 1979–1999*. Cambridge: Cambridge University Press.

Vanderlinden, J. 1996. *Anthropologie politique*. Paris: Dalloz.

Vansina, J. 1990. *Paths in the Rainforest: Toward a History of Political Tradition in Equatorial Africa*. Madison: University of Wisconsin Press.

Verchave, F.-O. 2000. *Noir silence: qui arrêtera la Françafrique?* Paris: Les Arènes.

Villalon, L., and P. Huxtable (eds). 1998. *The African State at a Critical Juncture: Between Disintegration and Reconfiguration.* Boulder CO: Lynne Rienner.

Vincent, J. 1990. *Anthropology and Politics: Visions, Traditions and Trends.* Tucson: University of Arizona Press.

Wagner, R. 1981. *The Invention of Culture.* Chicago: Chicago University Press.

Wagner, R. 1986. *Symbols that Stand for Themselves.* Chicago: Chicago University Press.

Wallerstein, I. 1976. 'The Three Stages of African Involvement in the World Economy', in P. Gutkind and I. Wallerstein, *The Political Economy of Contemporary Africa.* Beverley Hills: Sage.

Warren, B. 1980. *Imperialism: Pioneer of Capitalism.* London: New Left Books.

Waterman, C. 1990. *Juju: A Social History and Ethnography of an African Popular Music.* Chicago: Chicago University Press.

Weber, M. 1946. *From Max Weber: Essays in Sociology,* trans. and ed. H. Gerth and C. Wright Mills. New York: Oxford University Press.

Weber, M. 1949. *The Methodology of the Social Sciences,* trans. and ed. E. Shils and H. Finch. New York: Free Press.

Weber, M. 1961. *General Economic Theory,* trans. F. Knight. New York: Collier Books.

Weber, M. 1978. *Economy and Society: An Outline of Interpretive Sociology,* ed. G. Roth and C. Wittich, trans. E. Fischoff et al., 2 vols. Berkeley and Los Angeles: University of California Press.

Weber, M. 1985. *The Protestant Ethic and the Spirit of Capitalism,* trans. T. Parsons. London: Unwin.

Weigert, S. 1996. *Traditional Religion and Guerrilla Warfare in Modern Africa.* London: Macmillan.

Weiner, A. 'Cultural Differences and the Density of Objects'. *American Ethnologist* 21(2), pp. 391–403.

Welch Jr, C. 1995. *Protecting Human Rights in Africa: Roles and Strategies of Non-governmental Organizations.* Philadelphia: University of Pennsylvania Press.

Werbner, R. 1989. *Ritual Passage Sacred Journeys: The Process and Organization of Religious Movement.* Manchester: Manchester University Press.

Werbner, R. (ed.). 2002. *Postcolonial Subjectivities in Africa.* London: Zed Books.

Werbner, R. 2004. *Reasonable Radicals and Citizenship in Botswana: The Public Anthropology of Kalanga elites.* Bloomington: Indiana University Press.

Werbner, R., and T. Ranger (eds). 1998. *Memory and the Postcolony: African Anthropology and the Critique of Power.* London: Zed Books.

West, H. 2005. *Kupilikula: Governance and the Invisible Realm in Mozambique.* Chicago: University of Chicago Press.

White, G. 1996. 'Civil Society, Democratization and Development', in R. Luckham and G. White (eds), *Democratization in the South: The Jagged Wave.* Manchester: Manchester University Press.

White, L. 2001. *Speaking with Vampires: Rumor and History in East and Central Africa.* Berkeley and Los Angeles: University of California Press.

Wilks, I. 1975. *Asante in the Nineteenth Century: The Structure and Evolution of a Political Order*. Cambridge: Cambridge University Press.

Willame, J.-C. 1972. *Patrimonialism and Political Change in the Congo*. Princeton: Princeton University Press.

Willoughby, W. 1928. *The Soul of the Bantu: A Sympathetic Study of the Magical Religious Practices and Belief of the Bantu Tribes of Africa*. New York: Doubleday.

World Bank. 2000. *Can Africa Claim the 21st Century?* Washington DC: World Bank.

Wunsch, J., and Olowu, D. 1990. *The Failure of the Centralized State: Institutions and Self-governance in Africa*. Boulder CO: Westview Press.

Young, C. 1976. *The Politics of Cultural Pluralism*. Madison: University of Wisconsin Press.

Young. C. 1982. *Ideology and Development*. New Haven: Yale University Press.

Young, C. 1994. *The African Colonial State in Comparative Perspective*. New Haven: Yale University Press.

Zahan, D. 1979. *The Religion, Spirituality and Thought of Traditional Africa*. Chicago: Chicago University Press.

Zartman, I. 2000. *Traditional Cures for Modern Conflicts: African Conflict 'Medicine'*. Boulder CO: Lynne Rienner.

Zeleza, P.T. 2003. *Rethinking Africa's Globalisation: The Intellectual Challenges*. Trenton NJ: Africa World Press.

Zelizer, V. 1994. *The Social Meaning of Money*. New York: Basic Books.

Zolberg, A. 1966. *Creating Political Order*. Chicago: Rand McNally.

Index